D1396688

Peace at Daggers Drawn

Peter David Orr

PublishAmerica
Baltimore

© 2005 by Peter David Orr.

First printing

ISBN: 1-4137-4829-5
PUBLISHED BY PUBLISHAMERICA, LLLP
www.publishamerica.com
Baltimore

Printed in the United States of America

ACKNOWLEDGEMENTS

So many people are deserving of my sincerest appreciation in the research and development of *Peace at Daggers Drawn*.

On a personal level, my wife, Andrea, and my sons, Scott, Derek and Garrett deserve credit for so often being treated as a sounding board over the past eleven years. So often, and with very few complaints, they allowed me to expound on the vital elements of this work. Their patience and constancy over the years of research and development were essential.

I would like to express my appreciation to my parents, William and Sara-Jane Orr, and my grandparents, Frederick and Mary-Ellen Gerhard, for their financial assistance and encouraging spirit. They represent critical reinforcements to this effort.

Special homage is due to Dr. Howard F. Vos, professor Emeritus of History and Archaeology at The King's College. Howard Vos is an accomplished author and continues to be an inspiration. His support during my formative years as an aspiring historian cannot be overstated. I'm proud to count Howard as my mentor.

Professors Warren F. Kimball and Taras Hunczak of the Graduate School of History at Rutgers-Newark must be credited for helping to spark in me an interest in diplomacy and foreign policy as a historical pursuit, relative to the Second World War. Their critical appraisal of my original research and writing on this subject has propelled me to greater depths and a wider perspective.

A few institutions deserve mention for facilitating the research for *Peace at Daggers Drawn*. My sincerest appreciation is due to those who helped me at the Franklin D. Roosevelt Library in Hyde Park, NY. The same goes for the staff at the National Archives and Library of Congress in Washington, DC, and the Archibald S. Alexander Library at Rutgers University. The research staff at the New York Public Library deserves mention for helping me to track down some rare diaries and memoirs. Additionally, the creators of the New York Times Article Archive and the Avalon Project at Yale Law School are deserving of praise. These two projects must be mentioned, because they are on the cutting edge of bringing the history of diplomacy into the information age.

Table of Contents

INTRODUCTION

Long before World War II broke out over the question of Germany's right to regain territories filled with Germans in Poland, the Nazi-German leadership viewed war as a desirable eventuality. It was well known that Hitler would use the threat of war to make foreign policy. As far back as his first involvement in politics, Hitler had envisioned a war in the east against the Soviet Union—a "crusade against Bolshevism."

On the other hand, Hitler wanted peace. He wanted a peace that would give him a free hand to strike eastward in Europe. Practical reasons guided Hitler. A replay of the First World War, when Germany faced a two-front war, was to be averted. Hitler desired to avoid a war in Western Europe and once embroiled in such a conflict attempted to escape the consequences of the events he himself had set rolling by attacking Poland. The best evidence of this fact lies in what had always been the core of Hitler's ultimate vision of the future for Germany, Europe and the World—territorial acquisition in Eastern Europe.

The Nazi elite coveted the fertile expanses of Eastern Europe and felt it was their Manifest Destiny to found a Reich there that would make Germany a great power on the world stage once again. They envisioned a self-sufficient empire able to bestride the globe on an equal footing with the British, French, Soviet, and American empires.

Colonies that required a great and far-ranging navy would be renounced as a matter of foreign policy in order to avoid directly challenging Britain, France and the United States. Instead, living space and raw materials could be had for the German Reich by crushing the USSR.

A mythos arose among the Nazis: the belief that they were the saviors of western civilization. This belief system held that the leading nations of Western Europe would even be grateful to Nazi Germany for its services as the annihilator of the Bolshevik menace.

It was with conspicuous envy that Hitler coveted Britain, France, the United States and the USSR's geopolitical position in the world. These nations were first-rate powers because of the very massiveness of their territorial acquisitions. It was the mission of National Socialism to make

9

Eastern Europe a German colony. Rather than taming the "Wild West," the Nazis sought to establish an expansive Eastern European "ranch" of sorts. This Nazi foreign policy objective had been well established early on, with the Nazi leadership speaking openly and boldly on the matter. They did so even at a time when, militarily, it was nothing but a pipe dream. The Nazi world view implied the subjugation of the peoples and territories of Eastern Europe and perhaps beyond.

When Hitler first came to power in 1933, the political leadership of the world was already aware of Hitler's intentions. Not just Nazi anti-Semitism caught the attention of statesmen throughout the world. It was the Nazi world view, a Nazi vision of the future, that roused most foreign observers.

It was obvious what Hitler's "eastern-oriented" foreign policy implied for the security of Europe from the very start, because Hitler had come to power on certain promises. Even those who hated all that he stood for recognized Hitler as a man of action and iron determination. He made it a point to fulfill his promises. Hitler's domestic political popularity was mortally bound to his clearly defined goals involving the dismantling of the Treaty of Versailles that had ended World War I.

The destruction of the Versailles system was the Nazi Party's foreign policy priority. To do away with the treaty that so many Germans despised presented some serious obstacles to Hitler's "eastern-oriented" ultimate objectives. Germany would not be able to secure its place as a world power unless it could extinguish the limiting provisions of the Treaty of Versailles.

Dismantling Versailles necessitated a series of challenges to the will of the British and French to sustain its stipulations. Hitler planned to destroy the Versailles system systematically, over a period of years. He used an approach that alternated intense political calls for friendship and even alliance with Britain and France and blows to the structure and spirit of Versailles.

Hitler's diplomatic machinations reached a fever pitch in early 1939, when German armies occupied Bohemia and Moravia, which was at the time the only part left of Czechoslovakia.

Through British and French assistance and assurances, Czechoslovakia had been a first-rate military power on Germany's southwestern flank. Throughout most of the early years of Hitler's chancellorship the Czechs had a vastly superior military. Czechoslovakia was constructed with the designed purpose of helping to hem Germany in. Its existence was an integral part of Versailles as a security system. Nevertheless, Hitler was able to orchestrate Czechoslovakia's doom.

The German Führer borrowed from the "playbook" of the Western Allies who had defeated Germany in World War I. Hitler found that using one of the Western democracies' most popular post-World-War-I platitudes was highly effective. Hitler used President Wilson's phrase "the right to self-determination" to gain advantage in the repatriation of the Rhineland, the Anschluss (joining) of Germany and Austria, and then in the struggle to wrest control of the Sudetenland from Czechoslovakia.

Hitler took an idea that had been utilized to dismantle two German empires at the close of World War I and turned it on its head in order to create a single "Reich of All Germans."

The formula was simple, yet highly effective. Germans had the right to self-determination too. The Rhineland had been re-militarized by German armies because it was German territory. Austria had joined the Third Reich because they were Germans who wanted to be part of Germany. Similarly, there were significant borderlands in Czechoslovakia, commonly called the Sudetenland, that were populated by Germans, not Czechs. These Germans had the right to join the Reich. This territory, by the right of self-determination, should be joined to Germany. For this task, the leading political leaders of Britain, France, Italy and Germany met in Munich and worked out an agreement to despoil Czechoslovakia of the Sudetenland. It is in this context that Neville Chamberlain made his famous proclamation that "peace in our time" had been achieved.

By the spring of 1939, the inner turmoil of what was left of Czechoslovakia provided the excuse Hitler needed to mop up the rest of what he deemed to be an artificial hodgepodge of nationalities. Germany imposed a "protectorate" over Bohemia and Moravia and worked with Slovakia to establish its political independence from the Czechs.

Even as early as the Munich Conference on the Sudetenland problem, the same question had surfaced in Germany's relationship with Poland. This should not surprise anyone, since the same concept of self-determination applied to the 15 million Germans living in Danzig and the Polish Corridor. These populations overwhelmingly desired to be directly attached to the Reich. To this end, the Nazi-German government had been working on the diplomatic front for quite some time. The expressed desire of the German government to revise its borders with Poland to achieve territorial repatriation of these Germans in Poland was well known. Therefore, it was a common-sense development, which followed a logical sequence established over a number of years; first through the repatriation of the Rhineland, then the Anschluss of Austria and Germany, then in the case of the Sudetenland. Repatriation of majority-German-populated portions of Poland to the Reich was an obvious next step. Perhaps another "Munich Conference" could pull off a fair decision, with some teeth behind it this time around.

Yet something changed in the spring of 1939. Hitler had become *inconsistent* with his expressed foreign policy goals. Britain and France had facilitated the reincorporation of Germans into the German Reich in 1936, 1937 and 1938. It seemed morally untenable for the British and French governments to stand against a principle that they themselves had so often invoked as a prerequisite of geo-political justice. However, German actions in 1939 were remarkably different. Hitler had taken military action against the rump of Czechoslovakia and had established a "Protectorate of Bohemia and Moravia." Hitler's Reich now included *non-Germans* who had no wish to be part of Germany. This glaring inconsistency changed the western Allies' response to future German revisionism. It ended any future possibility of another Munich Agreement on the question of Poland's majority-German territories.

The Munich Agreement now took on a new character. It seemed painfully obvious that Allied "appeasement" had emboldened Hitler to widen his revisionist claims. There should be no more appeasing of Hitler or his schemes. Poland must be backed to the hilt. It should be encouraged not to give up any territory lest it be dismantled just as Czechoslovakia.

Despite the fact that the question of reincorporating Poland's majority-German-populated territories was a *long-standing* desire for revision on the part of the German government—now it looked as if it was a *new* demand by Hitler. After all, Hitler had announced publicly at the end of the Sudeten crisis that Germany had no more demands for territorial readjustment in Europe!

The reality is that the German claim on Polish controlled territory was nothing new at all. This claim had been announced as a German foreign policy objective back in 1934, when Hitler and the President of Poland, Pilsudski, had negotiated a mutual nonaggression pact. Despite this highly publicized fact, Britain and France now drew the line on any more territorial concessions. On the diplomatic front the British and French governments did everything they could to ensure the Polish government would refuse to negotiate with Germany on questions of territorial revision. There would be no more Munich Agreements.

Europe in the summer of 1939 was a powder keg. In the end, Hitler decided to use military force to achieve the repatriation of "German lands" held by Poland. Although the governments of the western European Allies and the United States had worked to stiffen Poland's resistance diplomatically, Hitler did not believe that these nations were willing to go to war over the issue. On this account, the Nazi dictator was sadly mistaken—or was he? Unfortunately, for Poland, the same governments responsible for getting Poland to be so uncompromising did not follow through with their promises of military support in the event of a German attack!

Hitler did not want war with Britain and France over Poland. The British and French governments did not want war either. They wanted peace but felt morally bound to guarantee Poland's right to exist.

So if neither side really wanted war; if all belligerents desired to avoid another World War, was there any chance that a general peace could have been negotiated after the Polish campaign was over? Once the Second World War broke out, were there efforts to conclude the war? What diplomatic efforts were made to bring a halt to the madness that would go down in history as the greatest slaughter mill of all times?

This work constitutes an original piece of research and writing dedicated to relating the diplomatic initiatives (both official and unofficial, public and secret) that were intended to end or stop the spread of the Second World War in Europe.

Special attention is given to specific peace proposals, initiatives, and back-channel diplomatic maneuverings, all within the general context of the intra-war foreign policies of all concerned parties. Diplomatic efforts designed to bring about an end to hostilities by belligerent and non-belligerent nations are included. Geographically, this work is confined to the European theater of operations. The chronological focus of this volume shall be on the earliest stages of the conflict, specifically from September 1, 1939, to September 17, 1940. It is the intent of the author to expand the time period covered by way of future additions.

CHAPTER ONE

The Failure to Achieve a Peaceful Solution After the Fall of Poland

Today, the war against England and France broke out, the war which, according to the Führer's previous assertions, we had no need to expect before about 1944. The Führer believed up to the last minute that it could be avoided, even if this meant postponing a final settlement of the Polish question....[1]

The Führer will try to use the impression created by our victory in Poland to come to an arrangement. Should this fail, the fact that time is working for the enemy rather than for us means that we will have to strike in the west, and do so as soon as possible.[2]

I believe Hitler also hoped the treaty [the Nazi-Soviet pact] would sober the west, particularly in England and France, forcing them to accept the aggressive policy of German imperialism. Hitler also probably hoped that France and England would write off Poland....He wanted to come to terms with the west and then redraw the map....[3]

FUNK: "I did not think that there would be a world war, otherwise preparations would have been quite different."
    Q: "Yes, but that means that you thought that you could have a war against Poland without the other powers interfering; is that right?"
    A: "Yes, certainly. And that was my personal conviction and everyone else's, that England would not start a war for the sake of Danzig."[4]

The Nazi-Soviet Pact

The factors which stood in the way of a compromise peace after the German-Polish conflagration are quite complex and require attention to the details of the diplomatic maneuverings between Germany and the USSR.

Understanding the impact of the agreement between Stalin and Hitler to divide up Poland helps to reveal why Hitler believed he could avoid war with Britain and France, even if he did attack Poland.

It should be remembered that the fateful decision to attack Poland only came after German Minister of Foreign Affairs Ribbentrop's diplomatic mission to Moscow and the resultant signing of the infamous Nazi-Soviet pact. This agreement took place within two weeks of the outbreak of hostilities. The officially published portion of the treaty between Germany and the USSR defined the signators' respective "spheres of influence" in eastern Europe. Of course, there was more going on behind the scenes. The attachment of a secret protocol involved the division of Poland along pre-drawn lines between Germany and the USSR in the event that war broke out.

On the German side of the equation, this pact was an attempt to guarantee peace in the west while military operations against Poland were taking place. Hitler and Ribbentrop believed that direct and timely Soviet participation in the dismantling of Poland would give the western Allies sufficient pause. The belief was that Britain and France would not declare war when faced with the prospect of fighting Nazi Germany and the Soviet Union. The secret attachment to the Nazi-Soviet pact was a diplomatic coup intended to keep the western Allies out of the war. Hitler thought that Britain and France had made official promises to Poland to sustain the Polish government's resistance to negotiations on the question of territorial revision. Hitler believed that the Allies would back down from declaring war in the end. Would they not see the utter foolishness of facing a war against a Germany free to fight on a single front?

Hitler gambled on the premise that the Allies would shrink from committing themselves to war under those circumstances. The German dictator and his leading advisors were convinced that the Allies would, as recent history indicated, put up all sorts of protestations; that they would be morally outraged; that they would probably be filled with a lot of brim and bluster—but no fight. Even though the British and French had publicly published their commitment to back Poland, and despite the fact that these three nations committed themselves to mutual assistance pacts, Hitler and his advisors held that the Allies would nevertheless climb down.

The *Other* Secret Protocol

What Hitler, Ribbentrop and other leading German statesmen were unaware of was that *another* secret protocol existed. Attached to the British guarantee to the Polish government was a secret provision specifying that any attack on Poland necessitated the declaration of war on *Germany alone.*[5] The British concluded this unpublished portion of their guarantee to Poland because they sought the USSR as an ally in order to make Hitler back down. If Hitler was trying to avoid a two-front war, then the best way of frightening him into a climb-down on threats of the use of force against Poland was for Britain and France to win a strong ally on Germany's eastern flank—the Soviets. Once war broke out against Poland and it was clear to the whole world that the Soviets were culpable on two levels, the British government's secret dealings were exposed. The Soviets had collaborated diplomatically to isolate Poland. Moreover, they had militarily participated in Poland's dismemberment. But where was the British or French declaration of war against the USSR? Of course, there was none. At least there was official moral outrage from London and Paris.

Practical reasons dictated the lack of a war declaration against the Soviets. The western Allies preferred to fight Germany—not Germany *and* the USSR. To fight Germany they needed a way to make Germany face the prospect of a two-front war. Allied foreign policy, dating back to even before World War I, was based on this premise. It was extremely difficult to articulate publicly a foreign policy that included a continued effort to woo the Soviets, so the western Allies decided to take a "hard line" on Soviet aggression against Poland while trying to avoid actions that might cause a state of war to arise with the USSR.[6]

Lebensraum and Continentalism

At this point, it is important to backtrack a bit in order to gain some perspective. There existed considerable division among Hitler's advisors on how to diplomatically deal with Britain and France. This division must be explored in its connection to the long-standing, "eastern-oriented" Nazi-German foreign policy. Above all, the notions of "Lebensraum" (Living Space) and economic "continentalism" are crucial concepts to understand.

Mein Kampf is the first place one can find Hitler's notion that one of two main pillars of German foreign policy must be the establishment of a strong friendship with Great Britain.[7] Below are some direct quotes from Hitler's infamous book:

> If land was desired in Europe, it could be obtained by and large only at the expense of Russia…. For such a policy, there was but one ally

in Europe—England.... Consequently, no sacrifice should have been too great for winning England's willingness. We should have renounced colonies and sea power, and spared England industry our competition.... Just suppose that an astute German foreign policy had taken over the role of Japan in 1904...there never would have been any World War.[8]

I openly confess that even in the pre-World War I period I would have thought it sounder if Germany, renouncing her senseless colonial policy and renouncing her merchant marine and war fleet, had concluded an alliance with England against Russia, thus passing from a feeble global policy to a determined European policy of territorial acquisition on the continent.

The most important consideration, first of all, is the fact that in itself an approach to England and Italy in no way conjures up a war danger.

The law of action would be in the hands of the new European Anglo-German-Italian alliance and no longer with France.[9]

Hitler's basic notions on this idea never changed. The same held true in the years after *Mein Kampf* was penned.

His attitude toward Britain remained unchanged in the fall of 1930. In 1930, Hitler spoke of a "return to a continental policy" and "collaboration with England." He related his willingness to "cede the ocean to England" in exchange for Britain not meddling in the eastern European affairs. This statement speaks for itself alone, but Hitler went further by proclaiming that a "treaty with Poland is the first step" toward a "consolidation of Central Europe." This "consolidation" would provide Germany with the platform from which to remove the "universal danger" of "Bolshevism." In that effort, Hitler prophesied, "England will even offer us help."[10]

It is not at all surprising to find that Hitler's negotiated nonaggression pact with Poland in 1934 was initiated at the same time that Hitler informed the British government of his desire to build a close bond of friendship. The German government made it known that it desired to come to an agreement. The British government was pleased to find that Hitler's government was making proposals to limit the growth of the German navy. Hitler was doing just what he said he would do from the earliest times—avoid a conflict with Britain by not challenging the lifeblood of her Empire. The German dictator hoped to avoid a naval arms race with Britain. Whereas Kaiser Wilhelm II had made efforts to bring German naval power up to parity with the British North Atlantic fleet, Hitler would agree not to exceed a ratio of one German ship to every six British ships (in all categories). Hitler wanted his actions to speak as clearly as his words. By signing the Anglo-German Naval Agreement of 1935, Hitler hoped to avoid committing what he believed had been the Kaiser's biggest mistake—the error that Hitler believed was largely responsible for causing the First World War.

After the Second World War, von Neurath, the German Minister of Foreign Affairs (1932-1938), reiterated to his American interrogators that the guiding principle of Hitler's approach to the west had been Hitler's willingness "to trade sea supremacy for [a] free hand in [the] east." Neurath also states that Hitler was ready to offer military assistance to Britain in the defense of its Empire, and that Hitler thought exclusively in "land terms" and felt that "colonies presented no ground for conflict."[11] Hitler did not want colonies in the traditional sense of the word. Rather, he wanted to make a large portion of eastern Europe into a German pale of settlement.

The Führer's thinking was profoundly influenced by the economic principles of Professor Karl Haushofer, the father of modern geopolitical theory. With Hitler, there was never a total break from Haushofer's "continentalism," despite the fact that it got him embroiled in a war with the British and French.

There are a number of other gems within the von Neurath interrogation by the US intelligence gathering team. Perhaps the most significant insight gained in the questioning of von Neurath is the claim that "Ribbentrop told Hitler only what Ribbentrop believed Hitler wanted to hear." According to von Neurath, Ribbentrop did not believe that the British would fight in the event of a military solution to the Polish question.[12] Ribbentrop was Hitler's post-1938 foreign minister.

Since Ribbentrop was von Neurath's successor, it is necessary to corroborate von Neurath's perceptions.

The Ultimatums

Dr. Paul Schmidt, Hitler's official foreign language interpreter, provides a valuable point of corroboration. Schmidt was present to witness Hitler's reaction to the reading of the British government's ultimatum, which immediately followed Germany's invasion of Poland.

Dr. Schmidt had the daunting task of translating the ultimatum in front of Hitler. Schmidt relates in his memoirs that Ribbentrop was present, and that when he was finished "there was complete silence." He continues that "Hitler sat immobile, gazing before him" and "after an interval which seemed an age, he [Hitler] turned to Ribbentrop" and with a "savage look" that seemed to imply "that his Foreign Minister had misled him....What now!"[13]

Even after Hitler was confronted with a clear ultimatum, he held to the position that no *real war* would be fought by Britain and France over Poland.[14]

Albert Speer reports in his memoirs that Hitler was "initially stunned [by the ultimatums], but quickly reassured himself and us by saying that England and France had obviously declared war merely as a sham, in order not to lose face before the world." Speer writes that Hitler ordered the Wehrmacht (the German army) to remain strictly on the defensive, citing that "if we on our side avoid all acts of war, the whole business will evaporate."[15]

An appraisal of Hitler's "Directive No. 1: For the Conduct of War" certainly reveals his mindset. This directive was dictated after Britain and France had issued their ultimatums. Specifically, subsection three of this order outlines that Hitler wanted to avoid hostilities with England and France. A document entitled "Top Secret Directive No. 2," issued the same day the Allied ultimatums ran out, reveals, yet again, Hitler's desire to step lightly in the hope that the war with Britain and France would "evaporate."[16]

Hitler's army liaison officer, Colonel von Vormann, describes the attitude in his personal diary, writing:

> This is just what we did not want. Until this morning, the idea was to play for time somehow and to postpone the decision [to use military force against Poland]. Even today, the Führer still believes that the western powers are only going to stage a phony war, so to speak. That is why I have had to transmit an order to the Army at 1:50 PM not to commence hostilities [in the west] ourselves. I cannot share his [Hitler's] beliefs. He has got the wrong idea of the British and French psyche.[17]

Keep it Quiet on the Western Front

Erich Raeder, who was the chief of the German navy at the outbreak of the Second World War, provides even more inside information regarding Hitler's thinking during the Polish campaign. Unlike Hitler, Raeder believed that the British were *absolutely determined* to prosecute the war. The German naval chief did *not* believe the declaration was bluff at all, so he attempted to impress upon his boss the immediate necessity of a stronger and more actively engaged navy. Raeder tried to convince the Führer that Germany should, at the very least, exploit its early advantages in submarine warfare. However, the admiral's arguments fell on deaf ears, because Hitler believed that a quick German victory in Poland would so strengthen Germany's position that negotiations for a new settlement with Britain and France would be possible.[18] It was Hitler's opinion that any naval losses inflicted on the

Royal Navy would *damage England's prestige* and *spoil the chance of a negotiated peace* with Britain and France.

Raeder admits in his memoirs that he was convinced for a time by the lack of serious British and French military action on the western front that such a noncommittal policy might work. The German naval commander claims that he issued orders to the effect that special care be given not to hurt commercial shipping. However, when this initial hope was rather quickly dashed by Britain's arming of all merchant shipping, Raeder writes that he once again tried to sway Hitler to lift the "shackling restrictions" that had been placed on the German navy. Even with mounting evidence of British determination to fight, Hitler was persuaded to unshackle the German navy "only little by little."[19]

The German dictator did some peculiar things when he believed that there was still a chance for a British and French climb-down. For instance, the sinking of the British ship *Athena* on September 4, 1939, by U-30 brought on an order from the Führer himself that the German submarines were strictly to observe the "Prize Regulations." This order stripped German submarines of their advantage. Germany's famous "pocket battleships" were "restrained" as well by a direct order from Hitler, so that the majority remained at home in port or in the South Atlantic—far from Allied areas of colonial interest.[20] An ironic corroboration of Hitler's restraining orders was British Prime Minister Chamberlain's lauding of the "victorious Royal Navy" on October 3, 1939. At a meeting of Parliament, Chamberlain praised the British navy because he could report that a whole week had gone by without an attack on Allied shipping.[21] Obviously, that was because Hitler was purposefully showing restraint.

Among the German leadership, Hitler was certainly not alone in believing that the war might yet be averted with Britain and France. After all, they had not made any serious military moves. There was not even a common feeling of animosity towards the British and French at the front. The most common banners posted by German soldiers in September, where their French counterparts could easily see them, proclaimed: "C'est à Votre Attaque Seul Que Nous Risposterons!"[22] When Franz von Papen visited the western front at that time, he observed French soldiers posting similar gestures.[23]

It was not just the average soldier at the front who desired an end to hostilities though, because the most prominent leaders of the German war machine were caught up in such hopes too. There was no real enthusiasm for war among their counterparts in Britain or France either. There were obviously some exceptions to this general trend on both sides of the conflict, but the exceptions were few. The vast majority of political figures on either side of the conflict were also for a swift end to the war. It surprises people

21

today to hear such a claim, but it is accurate. It is assumed that the Allied statesmen all knew the depth of evil they were up against and therefore were dead set against any notion of compromise with Hitler. Of course, it is assumed Nazis *wanted war*. These assumptions are based on what the war *became* and not upon the realities of the war's onset.

On this account, the French ambassador in Berlin's impressions are quite instructive. He attended Hitler's Reichstag address of September 1, 1939. Robert Coulondre made notes that he passed on to the French Ministry of Foreign Affairs about the address. What he reported reveals that the French government was aware that the war was far from being popular among the Nazi elite:

> It was noticed at this morning's session of the Reichstag that the Führer received the applause of the whole assembly only when he stated that he would fight like a soldier and that he would not wage war on women and children. Even then, enthusiasm was moderate. For the rest of the time, one-half only of the deputies applauded the Führer. The praises bestowed upon M. Molotov [by Hitler] found no echo. The atmosphere generally speaking, was rather dull. Among the people, although they still wish to cherish the illusion that this is merely a German-Polish conflict, today's events have produced nothing short of consternation.
>
> It is to be noted, moreover, that the Führer has taken pains to represent the action of the German troops [against Poland] as a police operation rather than as the beginning of a campaign, and that he avoided the word "war."[24]

Other evidence on the French side led high-ranking Germans to conclude that perhaps Hitler had been correct in his belief that the war would fizzle out.

Field Marshall Wilhelm Keitel recounts Hitler's anxiety over the strong and mobile Anglo-French armies stationed in northern France during the Polish campaign. These forces, Hitler worried, could make a virtually unchallenged foray into the heart of Germany. These Allied armies could have very easily made a "thrust through Belgium to break into the Ruhr." This attack, of course, never happened, but the threat was real. A successful attack of this sort would have meant an end to the German war industry.[25]

Yet when such a potential catastrophe never occurred, Keitel came to believe that, after Poland was completely overrun, England and France would make peace because "they would have no more war aim to fight for."[26] In addition to Keitel, Alfred Jodl admitted after the war at the Nuremberg Trials that he had been baffled as to why the Allies had not capitalized on their eighty-seven-division advantage over Germany on the western front during the Polish campaign.[27] The fact that the Allies did not take the war to Germany when they had clearly superior numbers on the western front led high-ranking German army officials to conclude that prospects for peace were strong as long as the German army did nothing provocative.[28]

Churchill in the Cabinet

Although Hitler and others on the German side thought that peace was still possible with the western Allies, the first real setback to the notion that the Allies had merely declared war to "save face" came with the British government's announcement of a new War Cabinet for Prime Minister Chamberlain. According to Albert Speer, upon hearing the news, Hitler had "dropped into the nearest chair and said wearily: "Churchill in the cabinet. That means that the war is really on.""[29]

Hitler's groanings were right on target. Still, despite Hitler's reaction to this news about the British War Cabinet, he had not yet been disabused of the notion that a negotiated settlement might be possible. Indeed, statesmen from around the world knew it too. US Secretary of State Berle's memo dated September 4, 1939, attests to that knowledge:

> I have some reason to believe that Hitler was furiously trying to establish contact with the appeasement group in [the] British Cabinet, and the defeatist group in France; but the tide was set. Fundamentally, Hitler's purpose was perfectly plain; he proposed to mop up Poland then "give peace," which is another way of saying dictate peace, to the other two.[30]

In other parts of the German government Churchill's inclusion in Chamberlain's War Cabinet spurred on the notion among a few well-placed individuals that the price of a negotiated peace might well be Hitler's head. Indeed, Churchill's uncompromising reputation aroused key members of the German general staff to talk secretively of the possibility of removing Hitler from power. They theorized that Hitler's removal might bring the western Allies to the peace table. This small band of conspirators carefully made contact with the British government through long-established channels. The German generals involved used prior personal contact with members of the British aristocracy in order to pass along their intent to make a move against Hitler when the time was ripe. To the conspirators, pulling off the coup was a matter of timing and trust. They had to be assured by their contacts that the Allies would not use the ensuing internal division in Germany. Were their contacts playing a double game—trying to split the German government asunder so that Germany's military defeat could more easily be facilitated? In the final analysis, the conspirators could not be certain of what would happen. They dropped their scheme for the time being.

While behind the scenes conspirators toyed with the idea of achieving peace at the price of Hitler's head, new developments in France complicated the situation.

The arrival of the British expeditionary force in France on September 10, Daladier's[31] formation of a French War Cabinet, the fact that the German defenses were only a "screen" in the west, were all contributing factors that encouraged a series of continued attempts made by Hitler to end the war with Britain and France. These events put the fear of defeat into Hitler. Could it be that the Allies might actually be seriously planning to prosecute an offensive war against Germany? The idea that the western Allies might launch an attack that the German defenses were not prepared to repel *forced* him to hope for peace! On the other hand, intelligence reports on the existence of certain elements within the French and British governments, which still were willing to negotiate a peaceful settlement with Hitler, did just as much to prop up the German dictator's delusions. Certainly, the diplomatic efforts by the governments of neutral nations must have helped as well, for these nations wanted to avoid a world war. They did not want to get dragged into the fight. Nor did they want to suffer the economic hardships that were certain to come as the major powers began to jockey for a better position. They wanted to localize the conflict, if at all possible.

The Initial Spanish and Italian Appeals

The first appeal for the conflict's localization came from General Franco of Spain only one day after the Allied ultimatums had expired.[32] On September 8, the Spanish ambassador to Berlin informed the German government that the French Minister of Foreign Affairs, Bonnet, "in view of the great unpopularity of the war in France," desired peace.[33] Since this is the same French politician that the German delegation had once heard repudiate France's Mutual Assistance Pact with Poland during negotiations in December of 1938, the German government took the report seriously.[34] German intelligence indicated that the Allies would soon be making a serious demarche and that Bonnet was going to initiate contacts to this end through Mussolini.

On September 15, Attalico (the Italian ambassador in Berlin) told the head of the German Foreign Office that Mussolini was in favor of "a really magnanimous offer of peace."[35] Mussolini suggested that Hitler offer overwhelmingly generous terms in order to facilitate an Allied climb-down.

So once again, Hitler seemed to have evidence of his suspicions that the Allies simply needed to save face in order to be cajoled to the peace table.

Hitler's Trial Balloon and the Soviet Dilemma

Hitler started toying with the notion of floating a trial balloon. The idea was simple: he would leak the news that he was willing to agree to the reconstruction of Poland with Allied input. Hitler could not come out and make a public proclamation of his willingness to negotiate the restoration of a Polish state because of the obligations he had already made to the Soviets. At the moment (September 19), it was more important to appease the Soviets than to make a "really magnanimous offer" as Mussolini had suggested. After all, the Soviets had started their attack on Poland just two days earlier.

The timing of Soviet military action against Poland was delaying Hitler's game.

The German government had signed the infamous pact with the USSR in order to escape a declaration of war by the Allies in the first place. The idea was that Britain and France could not *morally* declare war on Germany without declaring war on the Soviets as well—since the Soviet armies were going to join Germany in Poland's dismemberment. Such a declaration would seem somewhat hypocritical, would it not?

Hitler banked on what amounted to the Allies' "fear of the unknown." He posited that when the Allies saw that Poland's fate was certain and that Germany *and* the USSR had worked together to achieve this end, then the Allies would think twice about going to war over Poland. Hitler hoped that German-Soviet collaboration would give the Allies pause. He hoped that the west would be left with lingering questions and doubts, such as: what if Nazi-Soviet collaboration went *beyond* the dismemberment of Poland? Or what if the Nazi-Soviet pact included some sort of *secret military alliance*? However, a strategic delay on the part of the Soviets now threatened to undo Hitler's scheme.

Soviet troops were "concentrated on the [Polish] border"[36] on September 1, 1939, the day Germany attacked Poland. Strangely, the Soviets did not move into Poland in a *timely* manner. It was not *timely* from the German perspective, anyway.

When the Soviets failed to move into Poland right away as planned, Ribbentrop sent prodding messages to Stalin. The German foreign minister even went so far as to directly suggest a propaganda line that he believed would help to justify Soviet participation in Poland's demise. Ribbentrop recommended that the Soviets claim that they were coming in to liberate the ethnically Russian populations of eastern Poland.[37] Ribbentrop even went so far as to make a veiled threat, intimating that if Stalin did not take up his part of the agreement, *and soon*, a "political vacuum" in Poland might lead to the formation of a new Polish state in the portion of Poland that had been designated as belonging to the Soviet sphere of influence.[38] Still, the Soviets delayed taking action for another two days.

Why did Stalin Decide to Delay?

The answer is transparent: Stalin timed his participation in the Polish campaign to carefully meet *his* needs, not *Hitler's*. First, he waited to move against Poland until the Allied ultimatums to Germany had run their course. In this way Stalin made certain that the Allies would be able to regard his aggressive actions in Poland as a *distinctly different event.*[39] The more separation there was between the timing of German and Soviet aggression, the better chance Stalin had in avoiding an Allied declaration of war on the USSR. Next, he waited until the Polish government had escaped to neutral Romania. By the time the Soviet forces crossed Poland's eastern border he could claim that the government which Britain and France had promised to support—the same government with which the Soviets had signed a nonaggression pact—*no longer existed!*[40] This was *technically* true. By waiting, Stalin could technically claim that he did not attack the Poland that had received guarantees from the Allies.

The USSR was now in a better position to secure a *peace on their own terms*. The Soviets wanted peace, albeit temporary, to gain a strategic advantage in eastern Europe in a war that Stalin thought was inevitable—a "war of aggression against the Soviet motherland" by "the West." Stalin had faith that he would become indispensable to Britain and France again once Poland was out of the way. He knew the Allies needed him to hem Hitler in, and he certainly wanted to avoid a Nazi-German-led "crusade" against the USSR—a Nazi attack with the rest of western Europe looking the other way, *or perhaps even participating.*

Since Stalin wanted Poland out of the picture in order to engineer future Allied dependence upon his nation's military might, any notion of a "residual Poland" was out of the question as far as he was concerned. The Soviet Premier knew that Hitler wanted to use the idea of a rump Polish state, organized along strictly ethnographic criteria, as a 'bargaining chip' for negotiating a peace with Britain and France. However, Stalin made it known to the German government that he did not want *any new Poland.*[41] Whereas, the crafty Bolshevik wanted the war in the east to end so that he could begin to sure up his strategic position in eastern Europe, he also wanted tensions in the west to continue as long as he remained convinced that the Allies really just wanted to turn Hitler east. Stalin wanted the fires of discontent to smolder, but not go out completely. He called for peace publicly, but made certain to deprive Hitler of the one solid bargaining chip that may have actually brought the Allies around to negotiations. Now, if Hitler wanted the Soviet government's support in helping to facilitate a climb-down to the war in the west, the German dictator would have to tow the line. If the Nazi warlord really wanted peace with the west, Stalin reasoned, he could force Hitler into far reaching concessions regarding Soviet interests in eastern Europe. If anyone ever lived by the rule of "turn-about is fair play," it was Stalin. It turns out that *Stalin* pulled off the diplomatic coup de grâce,' not Hitler and Ribbentrop.

Stalin was convinced that he had turned the tables on both Hitler and the Western Allies. From his perspective the British and French foreign policies of the 1930s had a singular purpose—to turn Hitler east against the Soviet Union. Stalin did not view Chamberlain as an appeaser as much as an agent provocateur! Stalin was convinced by what he considered reliable intelligence reports throughout the 1930s that indicated that the British government, in particular, had adopted a policy designed to "turn Hitler east."[42] The Soviet dictator had looked for an opportunity for years to break the grip of the Axis menace, since it threatened the USSR with the prospect of fighting a two-front war against Germany on the one side and Japan on the other.[43] The memoirs of one of Stalin's top spies poignantly describe the Soviet government's perspective:

> The strategic goal of the Soviet leadership was to avert war on two fronts, in the Far East and in Europe, at any cost.
> The Soviet-German Pact was Stalin's master stroke to break the Anti-Comintern Pact. Yet it also indicates that Stalin did not want peace. If he had not made the pact with Hitler, he would have had a *de facto* pact with Britain against Germany.[44]

Stripped by Stalin of the possibility of offering up the recreation of Poland as a sop to bring the Allies to the peace table, Hitler had to seek out other options.

Even before all hostilities against Poland had drawn to a successful close for Germany, Hitler began a series of speeches, intended to prepare the way for negotiations with Britain and France. Churchill and others dubbed Hitler's calls for peace a "peace offensive."

The Peace Offensive Takes Shape

The German Führer's first important speech of this sort was given at the Guild Hall in Danzig on September 19, 1939. In the address, Hitler said that he had no interest in fighting Britain or France. Two key excerpts from the speech are in order:

> So, we have beaten Poland within eighteen days and thus created a situation which perhaps makes it possible one day to speak to representatives of the Polish people calmly and reasonably.
>
> Meantime, Russia felt moved, on its part, to march in for the protection of the interests of the White Russian and Ukrainian people in Poland. We realize now that in England and France this German and Russian co-operation is considered a terrible crime. An Englishman even wrote that it is perfidious—well, the English ought to know. I believe England thinks this co-operation perfidious because the co-operation of democratic England with bolshevist Russia failed, while National Socialist Germany's attempt with Soviet Russia succeeded.
>
> I want to give here an explanation: Russia remains what she is; Germany also remains what she is. About only one thing are both regimes clear: neither the German nor the Russian regime wants to sacrifice a single man for the interest of the Western democracies. A lesson of four years was sufficient for both peoples. We know only too well that alternately, now one then the other would be granted the honor to fill the breach for the ideals of the Western democracies.
>
> I have neither toward England nor France any war claims, nor has the German nation since I assumed power. I tried gradually to establish confidence between Germany and especially its former war enemies. I attempted to eliminate all tensions, which once existed between Germany and Italy, and I may state with satisfaction that I fully succeeded.
>
> That ever closer and more cordial relations were established was due also to personal and human relations between Il Duce and myself. I went still further, I tried to achieve the same between Germany and France. Immediately after the settlement of the Saar question I solemnly renounced all further frontier revisions, not only in theory but in practice. I harnessed all German propaganda to this end in order to eliminate everything which might lead to doubt or anxiety in Paris.
>
> You know of my offers to England. I had only in mind the great goal of attaining the sincere friendship of the British people. Since this now has been repulsed, and since England today thinks it must wage war against Germany, I would like to answer thus:

Poland will never rise again in the form of the Versailles Treaty. That is guaranteed not only by Germany but also guaranteed by Russia.[45]

There is much more to this speech than what is provided in the two passages above. Hitler goes into great depth in recounting his version of the events leading up to his final decision to attack Poland. This is the speech of a leader trying to drive the point home to the British and French that he now had achieved a fait accompli in Poland. The war with Poland was not entirely over either; although the Polish government had already "flown the coop," fighting would continue for nearly two weeks more. The point is that Hitler knew that the faster things could be wrapped up, the less chance there would be of the British and French attempting to escalate the war in the west. The speech was made to give the western Allies pause to consider what they might be about to initiate. Hitler wanted the Allied leadership to ask themselves two questions: 1. "Now that Poland has been defeated, can we really justify prosecuting the war? 2. "Is prosecuting a war against a Germany free to fight on a single front really such a bright idea?"

Observations on the Speech

Journalist and foreign correspondent William L. Shirer was in Berlin at the time and comments in his most famous book "all the Germans I've talked to" are "dead sure we shall have peace within a month."[46] A significant portion of the British and French populations seem to have been convinced that peace might be right around the corner.

So what was the reaction of the Allied political leadership?

Churchill admits in his postwar memoirs that he had known that Hitler had "not desired to continue a war with France and Britain" and that Hitler had "felt sure His Majesty's Government" would "accept the decision reached by him in Poland." The Lord of the Admiralty knew of Hitler's attempts to let "Mr. Chamberlain and his old colleagues" save face. However, Churchill does not stop there. He goes on to relate that "It never occurred to him [Hitler] for a moment that Mr. Chamberlain and the rest of the British Empire…meant to have his [Hitler's] blood or perish in the attempt."[47] Of course, Churchill was not in the "driver's seat" at the moment—Neville Chamberlain was still the British Prime Minister and he had an elaborate plan for achieving peace on better terms than Hitler was then currently offering. Chamberlain was considering peace, but only a peace when Germany was no longer in the dominant negotiating position.

Chamberlain's Peace Front Strategy

Chamberlain's way of attaining an acceptable peace in Europe involved five distinct stages. Proper timing and execution of his plan were required to carry it off. Chamberlain's plan was hatched some time during the first three weeks of the war. However, there appears to have been such widely ranging differences of opinion in regard to the future shape of Europe among the Allied leadership that it is certain that the plan took much longer to develop some "teeth."[48]

There is no way to be exact on the detail, because the records of the British War Cabinet meetings remain closed to the public until the year 2017. However, it is possible to extrapolate from the flow of events the fundamental outline of Chamberlain's plan. The following stages were envisioned:

1. Encourage internal political dissention within Germany on a number of levels, while making an all-out effort to destroy the German economy. The former was pursued because British intelligence reports indicated a high level of internal political dissatisfaction within the Hitler regime. The latter was to be achieved by the traditional naval blockade. Germany's international trade was, over roughly the next six months, to be significantly impaired. The Allies would work to deprive Germany of all avenues to foreign raw materials, especially those that would be necessary for the conducting of military operations.

2. Diminish and deflect the might of the German use of combined arms by creating a logistical nightmare for Germany. This involved getting Hitler to commit military forces to side ventures—in this way the strength of the German military in the eventual head-on fight would be significantly lessened. The idea was simple: this second phase involved spreading out the war. It was believed that if the war could be fought on territory that involved stretching the German war machine to the limits of its capabilities, perhaps the Germans might even find themselves faced with the reality that a head-on attack on French soil was no longer viable. The last nuance of the second stage would be an attempt to split the German-Italian Axis alliance.

3. After Germany had committed itself to unsustainable military forays and was duly strained economically to the point of internal collapse, then the time was ripe for the Allied armies to make a thrust into the Ruhr—Germany's industrial heartland. It was suspected that if the first two stages had gone as planned, stage three might even be unnecessary. The German government would most likely fall by an internal military coup, after which a negotiated peace could be actively pursued.

4. Make peace with a new German government—hopefully, one that had risen as an expression of popular dissatisfaction with the Hitler regime. If a more moderate regime did not come into existence, then Britain and France

would have to impose the break-up of the Reich into smaller, semi-independent states—something approximating the Confederation of the Rhine that Napoleon had created. In any case, the overarching principle was the achievement of a permanent disconnect between the Rhineland, Prussia and Austria.

5. Czechoslovakia and Poland were to be re-created on a pre-1939 framework.

Support, Internal Divisions and Unfortunate Perceptions

Chamberlain was supported to the hilt by Premier Daladier of France and most of his cabinet. The only person who consistently expressed grave misgivings about what Chamberlain called his "Peace Front" Policy seems to have been Winston Churchill. It was not so much that Churchill disagreed with the plan as it was in the proper *timing* of the stages. Churchill, for instance, felt that the tightening of economic screws and the spreading out of the war could be accomplished simultaneously. Churchill did not put nearly as much trust in the notion that internal political upheaval would arise either.

What is notably missing from Chamberlain's Peace Front plan? The Soviet Union. There is a simple explanation for this "oversight." The Allied statesmen were divided thoroughly on the issue. Some thought the USSR should be courted outright, while others were reticent to deal with Stalin. After all, the latter group argued, everything that Stalin was doing at the time was undermining the Peace Front plan!

In terms of the implementation of the Peace Front strategy, the Allied leadership were deeply divided. Compounding this internal strife was the fact that the leaders were not comfortable laying out the plan in public. They could not be transparent without completely undermining the strategy.

Unfortunately, this lack of transparency contributed to the perception that the Allies *had no plans for the future of Europe!* In addition, what the press in Britain and France could come up with was only bits and pieces of the plan, so the average citizen was left with the impression that no plan existed. Furthermore, due to these external appearances, Chamberlain's plan was exposed to endless "sniping" by its internal enemies. Churchill, for example, took full advantage of public perceptions to place Chamberlain under constant pressure to accept Churchill's modifications of the plan.

British statesman Sir Henry Channon indicates in his record of the war that the "glamour boys" were beginning intrigues again, and that "we [Chamberlain's circle of cronies] must watch out!" The Channon diary entry refers to the Churchill clique and its perceived undermining of Chamberlain's policy.[49]

The lack of public transparency of the plan also tended to foster the notion among foreign statesmen that perhaps the Allies might be willing to accept the "fait accompli" of Poland after all. Perhaps it was just a matter of time. Maybe the Allies just needed more time to "cool off." While the whole world wondered about Allied intentions, the Axis leaders were making it apparent that they wanted the war to end.

Mussolini's speech in Bologna on September 24, 1939,[50] called for an end to the war. Churchill publicly nominated Mussolini's speech as a second front of an Axis peace offensive designed to split the Allies. On the other hand, Chamberlain and Churchill thought that Italy might be eventually turned away from supporting Germany. It was part of the plan, after all. In France, the reaction to the Italian dictator's speech was similar. Nobody among the Allied leadership could be completely certain of Mussolini's motives. The suspicion remained that Hitler's and Mussolini's talk of peace was just a ploy to drive a wedge between the Allies in order to more easily "divide and conquer" when the time came for military action.

Enter "the Walrus"

On September 26, a Swedish envoy by the name of Birger Dahlerus met with Hitler and obtained his blessing as an official peace messenger to London. Dahlerus had taken it upon himself to be an independent peace envoy in London since the war's outbreak. According to the diary of Sir Henry Channon, Dahlerus met with Halifax and Cadogan on the afternoon of September 28, 1939. This peace envoy was not taken seriously by most of the British statesmen he encountered. Behind his back, these statesmen referred to him as the "Walrus."

Apparently, Dahlerus' official plea was not well received, for on September 29, he made a "personal plea for peace," which involved making Hermann Göring Head of State in Germany.[51] Dahlerus' suggestion was actually a ploy worked out between Hitler and Göring to see whether they could engineer a British climb-down by way of a feigned retirement. It was a backup proposal, planted by Hitler and Göring on an unwitting Dahlerus, intended to find out if the British government might accept this as a face-saving offer. Of course, the suggestion was not taken seriously, because the British political leaders knew that even if Hitler went into retirement, nothing would change. They would have to have been quite gullible to believe that Hitler's influence would go away or that he would remain "retired."

On the same day that Dahlerus made his "personal plea," Germany and the USSR signed the "German-Soviet Boundary and Friendship Treaty," which made a resounding joint declaration for peace. This declaration, along with the final disappearance of Poland from the map of Europe, made the French

32

government extremely vulnerable to overtures for peace. The specter of a war against the combined forces of Germany and the USSR was the primary element in this susceptibility.[52]

Before Dahlerus went to London, Hitler had expressed his pessimism to the Swede, saying that he just did not know how to make the British government realize that *he really wanted peace*. According to Dahlerus, Hitler was baffled by the British government's consistency in interpreting his offers as nothing but "pure bluff" or just "simple weakness." Unknown to Hitler, the British government *did* believe that Hitler wanted to get out of a general war. They just were not about to let him off the hook.[53] Most of the Allied leadership felt that a negotiated peace with a victorious Hitler was tantamount to signing a guarantee for a future war—on even more unfavorable terms. Therefore, the British government did its best to "sustain the French,"[54] even though it was a rather frightening prospect imagining that they might have to fight a war against *three* mad dictators.

While Dahlerus was in London, Hitler had various meetings with members of his government. One of these meetings was with Alfred Rosenberg, the Nazi Party philosopher. According to Rosenberg's diary, Hitler informed him that he intended to make a public appeal for an armistice and follow it up with a proposal for a peace conference.[55] Hitler indicated that he would take the fight to the Allies if his call for an armistice and peace was rejected. He made it clear to Rosenberg that he would launch an overwhelming attack if he felt he had no other choice.

Since Hitler wanted an end to the war, it is not surprising to find that the Allies were concerned with the German peace offensive that came at the end of September 1939. The British government was primarily concerned that Hitler might make some sort of offer that seemed *too sensible* to publicly turn down.[56] They had not yet enjoined the battle. Poland was already lost. To achieve what they thought would be a *lasting peace,* not just a temporary reprieve, they had to first sustain their will to war.

The Dutch-Turkish Connection

Two other peace feelers worthy of mention surfaced at the very end of September. Both picked up steam on October 1 and contributed to Hitler's mindset during the days in which he was deciding how to word his planned public proposal for an armistice and general peace conference. Hitler fed off information gained by way of these two offers of mediation.

One offer of mediation came from the Dutch government. This offer had seemed to the German Foreign Ministry to contain some promise of success due to the claim attached by the Dutch diplomat that the British were now "ready to negotiate." This lead came by way of Dr. Philip C. Visser, the

Netherlands' ambassador to Germany. On October 1, Visser visited Franz von Papen and revealed that his government was "willing to mediate in case an official wish was expressed." The queen of the Netherlands was willing to act in concert with the king of Belgium as a neutral mediator. Then, on the third of October, von Papen and Visser met again. In this conversation, the Dutch ambassador claimed that he had recently had "comprehensive talks" with the British ambassador to the Netherlands, Knatchbull-Hugessen. In turn, Visser passed the news to the Germans along with some official-sounding advice from Knatchbull-Hugessen for Hitler on how best to square his planned peace speech with the British mentality. Knatchbull-Hugessen counseled that Hitler should attempt to circumvent British public opinion. All official German peace feelers should go through confidential diplomatic channels first. Then, "for tactical reasons," the initial public offer "should be put in general terms without details, so that concessions which Germany was preparing to make could be used psychologically for the influencing of public opinion."[57]

This lead, as previously mentioned, originally came to the attention of Franz von Papen. According to von Papen's memoirs, he had passed on the idea, intended for the British government's ears, that the recreation of Poland was possible. He qualified this claim by saying that this new Polish state would not include Danzig or the Corridor (the areas inhabited by Germans). He passed this feeler on to London by way of Visser with Ribbentrop's blessing. In fact, the German foreign minister had hastened von Papen to the task—emphasizing that the British government might play a part in the recreation of Poland after all.[58]

Ribbentrop sent Franz von Papen to Turkey to follow up on this lead. However, to von Papen's dismay, in Turkey he discovered by way of Visser that "the British were determined for war," and that although these proposals were considered "suggestive of a move in the right direction," Churchill and others were now pushing upon Churchill *new* conditions for peace.[59]

William Rhodes Davis

The second of these two peace feelers was put into motion in Mexico and culminated in meetings in Washington, Rome and Berlin. It also seems to have had a profound influence on Hitler's peace speech.

American oil tycoon William Rhodes Davis was in Mexico in early September 1939, when he encountered German peace initiatives. Upon finding out what Davis thought was *inside information,* inside information that revealed a surprisingly reasonable attitude and a desire for an armistice by the German government, he used his friendship with John L. Lewis (then head of the CIO and personal friend of FDR) to arrange a private audience with President Roosevelt.

Davis had an economic interest in ending the war in Europe. He had been the broker of an oil deal between Mexico and Germany. This deal was now in jeopardy because it had been interrupted by the British naval blockade. Davis did not waste any time in heading back to Washington, DC.

On September 15, 1939, Davis met with Roosevelt and Berle. Berle attended the meeting because Davis was under suspicion of being a Nazi spy! Berle had warned the President of the possibility that Davis might be a Nazi agent, revealing that the US State Department had a dossier on Davis that went back ten years.[60]

Despite the suspicions, Roosevelt met with Davis and even ended up encouraging him to go to the Axis capitals as a peace envoy. Davis was instructed to find out Germany's peace conditions and to let it be known that Roosevelt was "prepared to use his good offices in initiating peace negotiations with the western powers if Germany assumes the initiative in this direction."* Roosevelt outlined three basic conditions, which were intended to encourage the German government to take the move:

1. Germany is to receive Danzig, the Corridor and all its former provinces in Poland, which it forfeited through the Versailles Treaty.

2. All former German colonies in German possession prior to 1914, currently under the mandate or control of other states, shall be returned to Germany at once.

3. To achieve economic equality with its neighbors, Germany is to receive financial assistance and the necessary raw materials and goods.

In addition to these conditions, there are a number of points, which Davis attributes to Roosevelt:

1. The President believed that Mussolini's attempts so far at mediation were inadequate in convincing the British to come to the peace table.

2. The US could apply the needed pressure within a short time frame.

3. Roosevelt had been opposed to the Allied declaration of war and had not been consulted on the matter.

4. He suspected the British of having "selfish, dangerous motives" in its declaration of war.

5. That neither the French government nor people wanted this war.

6. US economic assistance to Germany might be used as a threat to bring the Allies to their senses.

The President, according to Davis, wanted to be directly informed by Davis of the responses of the Axis governments during his mission. If the results were positive, the oil tycoon was led to believe that his next step would involve going on to London and Paris.[61]

The newly appointed, unofficial peace envoy embarked on a ship destined for Italy on September 20. On the evening of September 26, and into the early morning hours of September 27, Davis met with officials of the German government in Rome. This meeting provoked immediate transit to Berlin. The Italian foreign minister, Galaezzo Ciano, who was already interested in following up on Mussolini's peace initiative, went along with Davis to Berlin. Upon their arrival in the German capital on October 1, Davis met with Göring while Ciano met with Ribbentrop.

Davis related Roosevelt's desire to become a mediator in a peace conference, and, in turn, Göring made it abundantly clear that his government wanted an end to the war. Göring told Davis that Hitler's government welcomed the move wholeheartedly. Then the exchange focused on the necessity of flexibility on the part of the Allies over the recreation of independent Czech and Polish states. At first Göring stated that an "essential condition at this conference" [the proposed future peace conference] must be the acceptance of the fait accompli reached by Germany in Poland and Czechoslovakia. Göring admitted that he did not know what the boundaries of a future Poland would be yet. However, Göring felt that Roosevelt's proposals might create "a completely new situation." Hitler's second-in-command and designated successor ended the meeting by saying that he would bring everything discussed to Hitler's immediate attention.

On Tuesday, October 3, Göring informed Davis that Hitler would be making a speech on Friday, October 6. Göring told Davis that this speech should be interpreted as a direct response to Roosevelt's request for the German government to take the initiative. (see * on previous page). Davis was then informed that Hitler's speech could only embody a "general stand" due to Allied intransigence, but that "some of the points discussed between us [Davis and Göring]" would be included in the speech.

Then came what appeared to Davis as a stunning about-face by Göring. Göring told Davis that the German government would agree to the negotiated recreation of nation states for the Poles and Czechs. The German government wished for the US President to undertake mediation.

On October 4, 1939, Davis cabled President Roosevelt from Berlin with the following message:

YOUR VIEWS ACCEPTED HERE IN THEIR ENTIRETY, CONGRATULATIONS.[62]

The next day Davis met with Hitler and Alfred Rosenberg. At this meeting, the same points were agreed upon as in Davis' prior meetings with Göring.[63]

According to Davis, the Ciano-Ribbentrop meeting in Berlin had taken a similar course, with the Italians agreeing to "take no steps which would prejudice an amicable settlement of the present conflict at a peace conference, should such a conference take place."[64]

On Monday, October 9, Davis arrived in New York and proceeded directly to Washington, DC, expecting to see the President with all the details and good news. He was denied a meeting with the President but was received by US Secretary of State Adolf Berle and Jay Pierrepont Moffat. However, a lengthy letter survives that was written by Davis to Roosevelt. This letter, dated October 12, 1939, summarizes much of what he discovered during his mission. Of considerable interest are Davis' words on the possible creation of a residual Polish state. Under the topic of "Poland" are three snippets that stand out:

1. It is the consensus of those with whom I conferred that Germany would now be not only willing but anxious to bring about an equitable settlement with England and France, whereby a new state [of Poland] would be established. Germany desires to retain Danzig, the Corridor and Upper Silesia.

2. It is the general opinion of all with whom I spoke that Ribbentrop has made a tremendous mistake in the arrangement concluded with Russia.

3. Extended Russian penetration beyond the agreed-upon frontiers [in Poland] had complicated the prospects of a rump Polish state.[65]

To fully understand the significance of the last two of these three points, it should be remembered that Stalin was doing all that he could to *avoid* the creation of a new Polish state. This situation was in the process of changing while Davis was in Berlin. He did not know what else was going on behind the scenes diplomatically between Germany and the Soviet Union.

Back on September 28, the German and Soviet governments had signed another agreement. The German-Soviet Boundary and Friendship Treaty, that Ribbentrop had just concluded negotiations on, included yet another secret protocol. This protocol included a specific clarification of German and Soviet "spheres of influence" on the question of Lithuania and Poland. To make a long story short, Germany would cede Lithuania to the Soviet sphere of influence in return for the Soviet-occupied portion of the Province of Warsaw and the entire Province of Lublin, Poland.[66] This switch-up placed the vast majority of ethnic Polish territories in German hands. Now Hitler would have the territory needed for his coming proposal for a new Polish state—a Poland re-created on strictly ethnographic lines. Stalin was now giving Hitler his bargaining chip back. Stalin seems to have changed his mind. He was now willing to give Hitler the piece of property that the Führer believed was essential as a sop to the Allies. Perhaps, Stalin was not opposed to Germany, Britain, and France ending hostilities after all.

Hitler's Peace Speech

On October 2, the Belgian government made a renewal of their declaration of neutrality because of peculiar Allied military maneuvers on their frontier. On the next day, the British Expeditionary Force's First Corps took up a forward-looking position on the Franco-Belgian border. German State Secretary Weizsäcker saw Belgium's determination to defend her neutrality as a positive development.

In an official memorandum, dated October 2, Weizsäcker wrote about the impressions left on him by Jacques Davignon, the Belgian ambassador to Germany. Weizsäcker and Davignon talked over the possibilities for peace. Among Davignon's impressions was that "England is obstinate but that in France the cabinet even now still contains a number of pronounced friends of peace." This left Weizsäcker under the impression that these members of the French government were unable to assert themselves because of strong English influence over the French cabinet.[67] The German Foreign Office and Foreign Ministry were aware of the divisions within Allied leadership and recommended that this division be exploited in Hitler's planned peace speech. It was thought that perhaps Hitler could use this division in his speech to strengthen its psychological impact. Of course, from the Allied perspective, their internal division was something that had to be brought under control, for fear that Hitler might succeed in driving a wedge between them—all so much the better to divide and conquer.

Because of a divided French cabinet, the French Premier Daladier felt forced to assume a somewhat dictatorial approach in the decision-making process. Daladier had quite a diversity to deal with in the upper echelon of French government. On his right were the highly active French fascists; while on his left were the equally divisive French communist parties. Under this condition, the maintenance of any "war consensus" that existed in France required ever-increasing government controls on public information. Premier Daladier struggled to keep the French "appeasers" from going off the deep end and terminating the war prematurely. He agreed with Chamberlain that peace was desirable—it was a matter of proper timing and circumstances. Daladier believed that the Chamberlain Peace Front strategy was the best available option. He also agreed that the Peace Front plan could not function properly with these loose ends making trouble. However, the more conciliatory Hitler's tone became the harder it was to sustain the French people's will to war.

With such vulnerabilities in mind, the time seemed ripe for Hitler to pursue Mussolini's initial advice and to make a magnanimous offer of peace to Britain and France. What had been, at first, just advice from one ally, now was coming from neutral and belligerent sources. Moreover, Stalin had just handed him the piece of Polish territory that Hitler thought he needed in order to hold out the carrot of Poland's re-emergence as an independent nation. This convergence of events all tended to prepare the ground for a proposal for an armistice and peace conference. If Hitler waited much longer, he felt that the force of events could only work against him.[68] The dictator realized that even if his proposals were rejected, they would tend to sow the seeds of discord and, thereby, keep the Allies from prosecuting the war. The longer the Allies delayed in taking advantage of their early military advantages, the more time Germany had to make military preparations of its own. Therefore, it certainly could not hurt to make a reasonable public argument for ending the war.

Hitler's Reichstag address at the Kroll Opera House of October 6, 1939, was translated by the German Language Services into all important foreign tongues.[69] In the speech, Hitler stated that Germany had no reason or desire to continue the war against Britain or France, proposing instead a conference of all the major European powers in order to achieve an acceptable basis for future peace and security. Among the suggested topics of a possible peace conference Hitler listed disarmament, currencies, raw materials, and the nationalities problem. Near the end of the speech, Hitler presented "Churchill and his followers" with an ultimatum to publicly accept or reject his offer.[70]

The Nazi dictator's offer of peace was broadcast all over Europe. The actual wording was printed in the *London Times*. On the other hand, the French Premier, Daladier, did his best to censor Hitler's address.[71] Some newspapers, outside of Germany and Italy, actually took up the cause for the opening of negotiations, the two most notable being that of the *Hearst* article by David Lloyd George in which he called for serious consideration of Hitler's offer, and an *Izvestia* [72]article of October 10, which Joseph Goebbels regarded as Stalin's personal handiwork. This particular article called for peace and accused the western Allies of unnecessarily continuing the war. Yet another Lloyd George article in Beaverbrook's *Sunday Express* called on President Roosevelt to become "an honest broker in setting up a peace conference." Even George Bernard Shaw[73] published a highly controversial article that recommended doing away with "Churchillism" rather than "Hitlerism."

When surveying the abundance of good press on the speech one cannot help but recall the words of advice given to the German government, by Knatchbull-Hugessen, regarding how Hitler should best frame his peace appeal. It is worth repeating that the advice proffered by him was the same as had been offered in the previously mentioned Dutch peace feeler. The advice had been that a necessary second step in affecting a climb-down by the British government would be for Hitler to take his case for peace directly to the British public, through the press. An excerpt from a telegram from the German ambassador to the Netherlands to the German foreign minister speaks for itself:

> The Foreign Minister said to me today that British comment on the Führer's speech, both because of its careful formulation and because of the fact that Poland was not mentioned, seemed to him to be leaving the door open for a peaceful settlement. In his opinion it was now a question of easing the way for a shift in the position of the British government by conditioning British public opinion.[74]

The telegram then goes on to suggest that the next step on the German side to help the process along was to push to the fore the question of disarmament. The German ambassador to the Netherlands, Zech, who forwarded this message, even recommended that a special envoy be sent to London to open discussions on disarmament right away.[75]

One cannot help but recall what Göring had told the American peace envoy, William Rhodes Davis, just two days before Hitler's Reichstag speech. The German air marshall had informed Davis that, if Roosevelt wanted the German government to take the initiative, Hitler was willing to oblige. Moreover, Göring had emphasized that Hitler's speech, with an eye to English reaction, must be limited to broad strokes and suggestions in order to avoid the entanglements of premature specifics. It was thought by Hitler, and reinforced by the Dutch peace feeler, that mentioning specifics would stand in the way of opening dialogue. It is obvious that the articles that appeared in many newspapers may have been, at least in part, due to a full-blown peace offensive by Hitler—just as many of the Allied leaders suspected. The specifics were being leaked into the Allied press as trial balloons. These articles would naturally appear in the Allied press, listing the specifics in a way that seemed unconnected to the German government.

An example of what was planted by way of leaks made its way into the *New York Times* on the day before Hitler's speech. The article claimed to have a preview of the six major points that Hitler would be making. Revealing the source of this information as coming from "Nazi quarters," the article purports to give the reader a peek into the contents of Hitler's Reichstag Address. According to this source, Hitler's speech would include the following points:

1. Disarmament proposals. Hitler was willing to discuss all categories.
2. The creation of a Polish "national state."
3. "More liberties" for the Czechs.
4. Removal of trade restrictions.
5. A settlement of the Colonies issue is open to discussion and negotiations.[76]

Articles such as this in the British press releases in the first week and a half of October led the German propaganda minister, Joseph Goebbels, to comment in his diary:

> World opinion loosening up a little. Things no longer look quite so bad.[77]

The World's Reaction to Hitler's Speech

What *was* going on among the top Allied statesmen? What was the response to Hitler's suggestion for a peace conference?

Despite the Canadian Prime Minister's suggestion that Chamberlain should call on a committee of neutral mediators, the British War Cabinet, on October 7, thought in terms of "war aims" and not peace proposals. At least this has been the *official contention* of the British government for *decades*.

The official line is backed up by the diary of at least one individual present at these crucial, though yet to be open to the public, cabinet meeting minutes. Alexander Cadogan's diary reveals that the British government would not make peace with Hitler, adding that if Hitler could be removed from power, Germany would be in such disunity that they could not hope to win.[78] Cadogan's diary reflects Chamberlain's attitude in that the "war aims" were equivalent to his Peace Front policy. For example, Chamberlain wrote to Roosevelt on October 4, 1939, that the Allies would prevail "by convincing the Germans that they cannot win." The British Prime Minister did not believe Germany could even stand up under the pressure of the first stage of his Peace Front policy—relentless, international, economic pressure and isolation.[79]

The original reaction of the British War Cabinet to Hitler's speech was *not monolithic* though. For example, Halifax had said on October 4, in anticipation of Hitler's call for peace, that "unless it [the speech] is an overt humbug the Cabinet would give it careful consideration." In short, cabinet members *were willing* to entertain the idea. As long as these meetings' notes remain closed to the historians' prying eyes, one can only assume that the continued secrecy involving these minutes has something to do with the *depth* of these "careful consideration[s]."

At this junction, perhaps a sampling of reactions to the idea that Hitler was seeking peace is in order, so that a more full and accurate picture can be achieved.

On the other side of the Atlantic, the US Secretary of State, has this comment to make in a memo to Roosevelt written on October 6, 1939:

> Hitler made [the] speech in the Reichstag this morning. It purports to be a peace offer. It is, I think, the worst job of that kind I have ever seen done. Surprisingly enough, men who are as intelligent as Halifax are actually prepared to consider it to some extent.[80]

The US government was aware that the British government's response to Hitler's speech was not monolithic. It is not clear, however, whether the government of the United States was aware that the same differences of opinion existed within the French government. It is possible to get a glimpse now through the memoirs of the French foreign minister, Georges Bonnet. Bonnet indicates that high-ranking members of the French government discussed the idea of making peace with Hitler seriously. He even writes that the majority of the French diplomatic corps had indicated to him that they believed Hitler's offer "merited consideration."[81]

Winston Churchill was certainly among those Allied statesmen of the opposite opinion. The First Lord of the Admiralty had informed Joseph Kennedy, the US ambassador to Britain, that "any terms that might be offered by Hitler on a peace basis would be rejected."[82]

It is harder to be certain about Chamberlain's reaction to Hitler's call for peace, due to lack of documentary evidence. However, from what Chamberlain wrote to others at the time, it is safe to make the argument that he had more than less in common with Churchill. For instance, in a letter to his sister, dated October 8, Chamberlain writes that he was "anxious" upon reading Hitler's "clever speech," and that it "had been presented in a surprisingly friendly tone."[83] Chamberlain's use of the word "clever" indicates that he tended to regard Hitler's peace claims with thorough skepticism. Can anyone blame Chamberlain for believing that Hitler was pretending to be in favor of peace as a means of buying more time to prepare for war, or was using it as a way to split the Allied leadership?

Before the Allies made an official and public reply to Hitler's offer, Hitler spoke again of Germany's "readiness for peace" in the October 10 inauguration of "Winterhilfe."[84] Of course, this event was for public consumption. What did he write and say in private, among his military and political underlings?

Hitler's "Top Secret Directive No. 6," concerning the preparations of the army general staff, was couched in the following terminology:

If it should become apparent in the near future that England...and... France, are willing to make an end to the war.

This same sort of language is repeated in the secret memorandum Hitler used to introduce the necessity of preparations for the contingency of an offensive in the west. Hitler speaks plainly in the memo. It is clearly stated that there "would be no objection to ending the war immediately."

The German government, no doubt encouraged by William Rhodes Davis' visit earlier in the week, was waiting for Roosevelt's reaction to Hitler's Reichstag speech. The US ambassador in Berlin, Alexander Kirk, was asked to remind President Roosevelt that Hitler had taken the initiative, as requested. On October 9, Kirk let the US Secretary of State, Cordell Hull, know that Germany welcomed the idea of the President acting as a mediator to end the conflict. Once again, that Hitler would welcome a proposal for a "truce" from President Roosevelt was already a story found in newspapers in the US three days before the official reminder was sent.[85]

Roosevelt's Response

Roosevelt knew what Hitler wanted from him. The President remained publicly silent on the suggestion. Why did the President choose to remain non-responsive? Surely, Roosevelt never *seriously* considered acting as a mediator to end the war—or did he?

There can be no doubt that the President was partial to the Allied cause. The decision to remain silent was a joint decision made by the President and his senior State Department officers. The President's gut instinct was to remain quiet *until the Allies had taken the lead*. If the British and French governments sent clear signs of desiring his services he would then, and only then, break his silence and come forward with his desire to serve in the cause of peace. Roosevelt and his primary advisors conferred and agreed. They decided that it would be best to allow other members of the administration to be the mouthpiece for the decision. In the end, Roosevelt decided against making any proposal on the grounds that the timing might be embarrassing to the Allies.[86]

Rather than making any public pronouncement on the matter himself, Roosevelt assigned the responsibility of making the announcement to his White House Secretary, William D. Hasset, and Secretary of State Cordell

Hull. Hasset made the public announcement from the President's estate in Hyde Park, New York.[87] The President would not make any proposals unless he was asked to do so by the governments of Britain and France. Therefore, the entire world awaited the Allied governments' responses to Hitler's call to end the war.

Initial Mixed Messages from the French and British

One of the earliest Allied responses came to the attention of the German government in a rather roundabout way. A message from the Italian ambassador in Paris was passed on to the Italian ambassador to Germany, Dr. Bernardo Attolico, who, in turn, forwarded the text to the head of the German Foreign Office, Weizsäcker. The message stated that the French cabinet was now in favor of a peace conference.[88]

Hitler was immediately apprised of this encouraging report. He, in turn, had his Minister of Propaganda distribute new press releases (in Germany) emphasizing Hitler's desire for an end to hostilities. Particular care was given to these releases. Hitler and Goebbels came up with the wording of the release themselves, rather than leaving it to Goebbels' underlings, as was usually the case. The wording and tenor of the release was quite cunning—professing Hitler's sympathies for the French people and soldiers and proclaiming that he believed that neither he nor the French knew why the war should continue. Goebbels instructed his minions to push the story until they were sure that French newspapers had taken it up. Within a day, the major papers in France were parroting the lines that Hitler and Goebbels had personally crafted.

Sensing that the Nazi government's fingerprints were all over this latest peace offensive in the form of a media blitz, the French Premier, Daladier, moved decisively to gain control of the straying elements of his War Cabinet. He would present these wavering statesmen with a done deal. He decided to respond to Hitler's ultimatum to accept or reject the call for peace in public without consulting his War Cabinet.

Seizing the initiative, Daladier gave a resounding rejection to Hitler's call for peace on October 11, 1939. How could it be that the same government that had been described by the French foreign minister, just days prior, as being in favor of peace talks, were now staunchly against a parley? The answer is plain. It is impossible to describe the French government's position on negotiations as being monolithic. Daladier felt that he had to take action. He took the initiative when his advisors were indecisive, divided, and meddling behind his back. The only other plausible explanation for why members of Daladier's government had been signaling the German government that they were ready to negotiate is that they were doing precisely what they thought Hitler might be doing— stringing Hitler on just enough to make *him* indecisive; just enough to give *him* pause; just enough to drive a wedge between *him* and the Italians.

On the same day, behind the scenes in the British higher echelon, "Rab" Butler was told by Cadogan and the "Secretary of State" that Chamberlain's response to Hitler's call for peace would be "almost, but not quite, a definite refusal of Hitler's terms."[89] On this point, the official line from the British government has been that they never for a moment contemplated the notion of accepting Hitler's offer. So, why was there a delay of several days? The official answer has always been that the six-day delay was due to the War Cabinet's careful consideration of the *form* that the reply should take.

The decision was taken to have Chamberlain make a rejection couched in unanswerable questions. In a letter from Neville Chamberlain to the British ambassador in Washington, Lord Lothian, the Prime Minister later admitted that the intent of his official reply was to state peace conditions that "Hitler would find impossible to accept."[90]

Chamberlain's Official Response

Chamberlain made his response to Hitler's offer before Parliament on October 12, 1939. The careful wording of this address makes Chamberlain's goal clear: Hitler would be given just enough hope in the speech. Just enough hope to perhaps delay Hitler's current rush of troops to the western front. Time was needed in order to set up the first phase of Chamberlain's Peace Front policy. It was too early to call for peace, when insufficient time had gone by in order to gauge the effectiveness of phase one—the economic pressure on Germany was just then getting under way. Perhaps in a few months' time Hitler would be in a much different position. Perhaps the Hitler regime could be brought to its knees without unnecessary bloodshed. If Germany could be brought to doubt the necessity of a winter offensive, by the spring Germany's economy, and with it the Hitler regime, would be in shambles. Leading Hitler and his advisors on by sending mixed signals was a brilliant strategy.

In addition, Chamberlain believed that time was needed to shift the alliance situation in Britain and France's favor—especially since the Soviets had become so unpredictable in recent days. As early as October 4, the British cabinet was considering sending Sir Stafford Cripps to Moscow to work on re-establishing more amicable relations, Churchill being the most outspoken proponent.[91]

Chamberlain could now breathe a sigh of relief. His Peace Front policy seemed to have survived the first German peace offensive. The Prime Minister's strategy had survived, in no small part due to Roosevelt's keen understanding of the situation. The United States, which many had expected would come in as an impartial mediator and help to put an end to the war, was willing to wait on taking any initiative in that direction before the Allies were ready. The decision made in Washington helped to sustain Chamberlain's objectives and to keep the Allied governments from being internally divided any more than they already were.

The Neutrals Scramble to Pick off the Pieces to No Avail

The rejection of Hitler's peace offer set the smaller neutral nations aflame with renewed offers of mediation. The neutral nations knew what was ahead for them. They wanted to stay out of the war. They did not want to be indirectly drawn into taking sides either. Even though the war was not heating up, the pressure to join sides due to economic necessities was increasing daily. Offers came pouring into Ribbentrop's office from Spain, Italy, Norway, Finland, Holland, and countless other *unofficial* American sources.[92] Then, on the fourteenth of the month, in a telegram from Neuhause (the German chargé d'affaires in Norway), Ribbentrop's office received a report that the Scandinavian kings were all jointly willing to sponsor a peace initiative.[93] This initiative met a dead end in Paris, London and Berlin.

On October 15, Ribbentrop notified the German legation in Finland that, due to Chamberlain's rejection of Hitler's "magnanimous peace offer in the most insolent manner," the issue of "peace" was closed as far as he was concerned.[94] When this Ribbentrop statement became official German foreign policy on October 18, all the neutral nations were notified.[95]

Hitler Fails to Quickly Squelch the Rumors

If Hitler set all thoughts of peace with the west aside after his proposal was rejected, he did not lead the German people to believe so. The failure to dispel any idea of peace among the German people seems uncharacteristic of a dictator who always thought to work on the will of the people first. Letting unrealistic rumors of a possible peace run rampant was not an intelligent *propaganda* move to make in terms of sustaining the German people's "will to war." Even the German master of propaganda, Joseph Goebbels, did not take action to quell reports in the German press about peace prospects. German newspapers carried stories of peace initiatives in the days following Hitler's peace speech without the Minister of Propaganda lifting a finger to stop them. The reports and rumors were not helpful to the "fighting spirit" of the German people. They lived under the illusion that peace was just around the corner for over two weeks.

Was it just that Goebbels bungled a major chance to stick it to the Allies? After all, it seems as if he should have been attacking the Allies as "warmongers" and such. So, why did he refrain? Was it not Goebbels job to put backbone into the German population in light of an impending war of aggression as planned and marshaled by his Führer? Why was he doing the direct opposite? Perhaps, he was just plain outfoxed.

According to famous American journalist William L. Shirer's diary, the German press had launched another peace offensive on October 10. The German press "mistakenly" reported that the British government had fallen and that there would be an armistice.[96] The German public was overjoyed at the thought. Word of the reaction of the German public reached the Assistant Secretary of State's attention immediately. Berle wrote in his diary that:

> The most dramatic matter of the day so far is the news of what happened in Germany when a rumor was spread that there was armistice. If you believe the Berlin report the population went almost crazy with joy.[97]

In an attempt to calm the public down, the evening edition of many German newspapers ran front-page stories about how the British Secret Service had "played a dirty trick on the German people by starting rumors of peace."[98] Perhaps Goebbels had been outsmarted.

The German Minister of Propaganda's daily log of October 12, 1939, reads, "Whether it will come to a real world war? No one can say yet."[99] This entry was made *the day after* the German press had published the misleading story that peace was at hand. Goebbels was coming to terms with the subtle nuances of a "phony war." A war of words and endless jockeying for advantage was beginning. His and his boss's personal hopes were blinding them from getting on with the game at hand. Nevertheless, he was beginning to catch on. Goebbels' diary reveals his analysis of current events and his decision to change his propaganda tactics—the press lines to be sown in order to engineer an Allied climb-down while not destroying the German population's "will to fight." The decision was made to attack the warmongering wire-pullers in the British and French government. For example, Churchill was to be the target, not the British government, not the British people. The intent was to preserve the integrity of a future government who might be willing to bury the hatchet. A confirmation of this interpretation is found in Goebbels' diary entry of October 14, 1939.

The U-47's sinking of the *Royal Oak* at anchor in Scapa Flow caused Goebbels to scratch angrily down that "the irresponsible attitudes to be found in certain departments [the German navy] must be partially to blame for the prolongation of the war."[100] The reasons to be upset with the German navy are obvious, but Ribbentrop's actions might have been even more damaging to Germany's chances for ending the war.[101] Ironically, Hitler had to straddle the fence. To keep up the morale of his daring submariners he immediately called Gunther Prien, the commander of U-47, to Berlin to present him with honors. At the same time he let the naval brass know of his acute displeasure. This was certainly no way of allowing the British to save face!

After the war, many of the captive Germans of high rank pointed an accusing finger at Ribbentrop. Many held Ribbentrop responsible for exercising a "great and sinister influence" on Hitler. The German foreign minister had been "a rabid enemy of Great Britain" in the opinion of many German statesmen.[102] Under Allied interrogation, after the war, the head of the German Foreign Office indicated that the removal of Ribbentrop would have helped to clear other obstacles standing in the path of a peaceful solution.[103]

Corroboration of these impressions can be found in the von Papen memoirs, which show that Ribbentrop *purposely kept information about peace prospects from Hitler.* On one occasion, when von Papen thought that he had discovered an extremely positive lead in the quest for a peaceful solution, he had turned to Göring in order to circumvent Ribbentrop. He hoped to bypass Ribbentrop by way of Göring. However, Goring told von Papen, at the time, that he could no longer get through to Hitler, because he "and Ribbentrop had made up their minds to have it out with Britain."[104]

On October 18, a break in Germany's internal policy of seeking a peaceful solution occurred. Ribbentrop seems to have taken the lead role in convincing Hitler to move on. Ribbentrop was convinced by then that the peace feelers from Britain and France were nothing more than a cleverly designed ploy to slow down German preparations for prosecuting the war.[105] The only way to end the war, as far as Ribbentrop was concerned, was a quick defeat of the Allied armies gathering in France. Ribbentrop's speech of October 25, 1939, was "universally acknowledged as the final break."[106]

Poland's Demise: War Without Armistice, War Without End.

In the search for documentary evidence on the ending of hostilities in the Polish campaign of 1939, a curious oddity was uncovered. Where were the documents detailing the Polish government's surrender? Where were the documents of the German-Polish armistice? Any research addressing the question of peace prospects in the midst of the Second World War would have to include analysis of the cessation of hostilities and the ensuing negotiations that must have taken place between representatives of the German and Polish Armed Forces and governments. The search seemed futile. There was no armistice to be found. Negotiations? What negotiations?

The search turned up only evidence that Poland's government was mysteriously absent.

The Polish government had fled the country. President Moscicki and the chief members of his government had escaped across the Polish-Romanian border one day before that boundary was sealed by the Soviet onslaught on eastern Poland. By that time, Warsaw was hopelessly surrounded by the German army. The Polish forces in this pocket put up a heroic struggle—only to be decimated by aerial bombardment in the end. The remnant retreated to Warsaw for one last stand. The surrender of Warsaw came by way of a cease-fire plea. A call for mercy by Warsaw's mayor, Stefan Starzinsky[107] and the commander of Warsaw's defenses, General Juliusz Rómmel, was forwarded to the surrounding German army. Accepting or rejecting the offer of surrender fell to the Commander in Chief of Germany's armies in Poland, General Johannes Blaskowitz. On September 27, 1939, Blaskowitz accepted the unconditional surrender of the city and its defenders. The war with Poland was now over—or was it?

What is the explanation for the curious absence of Poland's government? The answer is quite shocking.

The reason can be found in the text of the Mutual Assistance Pact signed by the Polish and British and French governments. Note well the wording of Article VII within the Anglo-Polish Mutual Assistance Pact:

> Should the contracting parties be engaged in hostilities in consequence of the application of the present Agreement, they will not conclude an armistice or treaty of peace except by mutual agreement.[108]

The answer is thoroughly shocking, because the Allied governments hung Ignace Moscicki's government out to dry! The Allies had not prosecuted the war against Germany on the western front, while Poland was going under, even though they had promised to do so. Then, when Poland's armies were beyond help, and the Polish government might have retained, at the very least, some flexibility in order to face the German victors as the representatives of a sovereign government, the Allies would not allow the Polish government to escape its previous commitment not to make a separate armistice or peace.

Instead, the British government worked behind the scenes to facilitate the Polish government's escape, by way of Romania.[109] The remnant that would make it to London eventually on board a British man-of-war was to be established as Poland's official government in exile.

On September 30, 1939, three days after Warsaw's capitulation, the Polish ambassador to Britain, Edward Raczynski, proclaimed from London in "the name of the Polish government" that "Poland will never recognize this act of violence" and "will not cease to struggle" until "her legitimate rights will be established in their entirety."[110]

If the British had secured a Polish government in exile, then what was stopping Germany from pursuing a copycat venture? If Hitler thought he might be able to use the prospect of a residual Poland as a sop to the Allies in negotiation to end the war in the west, then it would make sense that there must have been some effort in this direction.

In point of fact, Hitler was contemplating the idea of creating a residual Polish state. This state would be reconstructed along strictly ethnographic lines. Its shape would approximate that of the Kingdom of Poland set up by the German government during the First World War. The German military administration under Gerd von Rundstedt and the civilian administration of the German-occupied portions of Poland headed by Hans Frank, as set up on September 25, 1939, was done in keeping with international law.[111]

It is not surprising that the German government pursued individuals who had collaborated with Germany during World War I. A number of Polish politicians were courted, including Prince Janusz Radziwill, Count Adam Ronikier, Professor Wladyslaw Kucharzewski, and publicist Wlakyslaw Studnicki. However, by the time that serious effort was being made to construct a residual Poland, it had already become abundantly clear that its creation would not have the desired effect. It was decided on the same day that Ribbentrop made his speech marking the end of the German government's policy on seeking a peaceful solution with the west, October 25, that the plan to create a new Polish state was put on hold. The military administration of Poland was ended at the same time as Gerd von Rundstedt was called into service in the planning and carrying out of the war against Britain and France.

According to Ulrich von Hassel's diary entry of October 19, 1939, Hitler ordered all peace feelers emanating from German sources to be halted. Only peace proposals initiated by the Allies would henceforth be considered.[112] Thus began the next phase of the German government's policy of intransigence, which lasted up to May 10, 1940.

CHAPTER TWO
"No Patched-Up Peace!" The Welles Mission and the Period of Intransigence.

Goebbels' diary entry of Oct 25, 1939:

> The English are drawing the wrong conclusion. The more we talk of peace, the longer the war will last. These days showing nothing but intransigence.[113]

The Finnish ambassador to Great Britain (Grippenberg) remarks in his memoirs:

> During those days one could occasionally hear criticism, even by sensible and responsible men in the city [London] and in other cities, of Chamberlain's and Halifax's "intransigence," of their refusal even to listen to Hitler.[114]

Chamberlain's response to a confidant who counseled peace in late January 1940:

> Your letter is a plea for peace at any price...if we were prepared to pay any price we could get peace for a time. It would, however, be only for a time.[115]

51

US Assistant Secretary of State Adolf Berle's memo of December 26, 1939:

> My private opinion is that the President is working towards trying to summon a general peace conference before the beginning of the spring drives. My own mind is leaning in that direction. I agree that this will not be ideal. But I do not see that it will be any more ideal, no matter who comes out top dog in the spring and summer fighting.[116]

Adolf Berle's diary concerning the Welles Mission to Europe:

> Well, the fact of the matter is that nobody knows what Welles is doing. He cables in cipher to the President, and even the Secretary does not get these reports.[117]

Intransigence

By the last week of October 1939, a mood of intransigence characterized relations between the belligerents. The German and Allied governments became intransigent as a matter of policy. The official attitude that developed on each side of what has become known as the "Phony War" was distinctly different on each side of the Siegfried and Maginot Lines. This intransigence was caused by each side's desire to maintain a perceived position of advantage for the future, whether the days ahead held war or peace. To a degree, the intransigence was just simple posturing. A stagnant war of bluff, to gain the best possible advantage for the time the war finally heated up. On the other hand, the desire for a climb-down was still genuinely felt by statesmen on both sides of the impending bloodbath.

On the outskirts of belligerence, the three great neutral nations played a major role in affecting perceptions of an acceptable future peace—a peace "for when the time comes," so to speak. Italy, the Soviet Union, and the United States' part in the shaping of war and peace attitudes should not be underestimated.

The Soviet Role in the Period of Intransigence

The Soviets played a major part in the question of "what sort of war" was to continue because of Stalin's desire to avoid being used as a shock absorber of Allied policy.[118] To Stalin, this desire had justified the Nazi-Soviet pact. He had bought a temporary peace by turning Hitler west. In the general context of peace proposals during the period of the Phony War there are ramifications of the Nazi-Soviet pact that have hardly been touched upon by other histories of the period. The Nazi-Soviet pact deserves closer scrutiny, as it was a significant factor in the period of intransigence.

By way of this pact, the Soviets had erased the barrier that kept their troops from direct access to Germany. The dismemberment of Poland had placed the Soviets in a better bargaining position with the Allies as well as Germany. The USSR had achieved a better position when it came to influencing the future shape of eastern Europe in particular. However, the Soviets still had a complicated dilemma. They knew that Hitler had always wanted a war with the "Bolshevik menace" rather than the war with the western Allies in which he presently found himself. Stalin knew what the Nazi world view was. He understood the implications of that world view to German foreign policy. He took Hitler's previous proclamations at face value. Behind Stalin's well-founded instincts on Hitler's future intentions was his lurking distrust of the British and French governments. It seemed to the Soviet Premier that Allied foreign policy over the past 6 years had been designed to turn Nazi Germany loose against the USSR.[119] Hitler had to be turned west! The Nazi-Soviet pact enabled Stalin to engineer a situation in which his government could work for both war and peace between Nazi Germany and the western Allies. The USSR had become indispensable to both.

When the war between Germany, Britain and France did not end, Stalin counted on a drawn-out war, the sort of war in which only the USSR could really profit. However, the Phony War did not fit neatly into the world of Stalin's prognostications. The war did not end after the demise of Poland, nor did it begin in earnest in Western Europe. As two distinct varieties of intransigence developed over a longer-than-average European winter, the Soviets attempted to take advantage of their unique position. In a series of diplomatic initiatives, the Soviet foreign minister, Molotov, gained unprecedented strategic access all across eastern Europe. The Soviets took full advantage of the Nazi-Soviet pact and its general references to German and Soviet "spheres of influence" in eastern Europe to negotiate economic and military-transit agreements. Soviet pressure on their eastern-European neighbors now worked wonders since Germany was no longer exerting diplomatic influence on these nations to *resist* Soviet demands. Germany obviously had other, more important concerns. Soviet policy in eastern Europe met stiff resistance in Europe only in Finland. Finnish resistance to Soviet demands for strategic territorial adjustments with Finland led to war—the Russo-Finnish War, also known as the "Winter War."

Not unconnected to the shock waves felt over the Winter War sideshow, was the role the United States played in the maintenance of the Allied and German versions of intransigence. In particular, the mission of US Undersecretary of State Sumner Welles to Europe in February–March of 1940, presents one with an opportunity to examine peace prospects within the context of intransigent attitudes. Within the Welles mission were tied up all the important notions of what war and peace meant to belligerent and non-belligerent nations alike. The Welles mission was a curve ball in the midst of a high-velocity game of war preparation—of gathering the will and energy to break away from the months of inactivity and bring matters to a head. While the belligerents had now decided to get down to serious planning concerning how to best take the fight to the enemy, this peace envoy and his peculiar mission threatened the intransigent assumptions held on both sides. Just when both sides felt they were gaining the diplomatic upper hand for the coming spring offensives, Welles appeared on the scene. President Roosevelt's decision to send Sumner Welles to Rome, Berlin, Paris and London rekindled all the former doubts of the earliest stage of the war—September 1, 1939, to October 25, 1939.

The Welles mission was profoundly disturbing to the combatants. The last thing they wanted was for there to arise any divisions between the war partners. Britain and France had struggled to get on the same page to begin with, on the one side. On the other side, Germany did not have a commitment from its Axis partner to join in the fight when the time came.

Hitler and Ribbentrop had envisioned, before the decision to attack Poland, that, even if a worst-case scenario developed and Germany was faced with a declaration of war by both Britain and France, at least their Italian ally would stand by their side. Having the Italians live up to the prior agreement made with Germany in their Pact of Steel was something that Hitler had taken for granted. Hitler assumed that Mussolini's government would stand by Germany's side and in doing so would give the Allies additional pause when it came to initiating any real military action.

Dr. Paul Schmidt, Hitler's interpreter, related to his American interrogators after the war that the "deepest resentment prevailed in Germany toward Italy" when Mussolini failed to stand side by side with Hitler against Britain and France.[120] He also writes, "Ribbentrop cherished a theory that a member of the House of Savoy must have intimated to the British Royal House that Italy would not become belligerent and that Britain, only after it had received this information, signed the treaty with Poland."[121]

The Italian government had decided not to claim that the terms of the Pact of Steel did not apply to the current situation for two reasons:

1. Since Hitler did not want war with Britain or France, Mussolini thought that remaining neutral would be more useful. Mussolini did not want war with the Allies either. Perhaps, his "good offices" would be needed as a mediator, as had been the case during the German-Czechoslovakian crisis over the Sudetenland.

2. Mussolini was upset with Hitler's dealings with the Soviets. The very idea of striking a deal with the Bolsheviks was repugnant to Mussolini. The Duce could not help but wonder if the new Nazi-Soviet pact carried with it provisions that would tend to work against Italy's interests in southeastern Europe.

Mussolini wanted the war to end as soon as possible. He did not want Italy dragged into the war. Moreover, he could not stomach the notion of cooperation with an enemy that he was convinced would never change his stripes, so to speak.

As the period of intransigence began, Germany still had an official ally in Rome. However, would Italy come to Germany's assistance if the war heated up? The German government really could not be certain of Italy joining in the war against Britain and France. Even more disconcerting to the German government was the idea that the division within the Axis partnership could be further exploited. There can be no doubt that the specter of Italy's switching of sides, as they had during the First World War, haunted the Germans. When President Roosevelt announced his intention to send Undersecretary of State Sumner Welles to Europe, the German government suspected that Welles' "peace mission" was really a sinister ploy to exploit the divisions that had developed between Nazi Germany and Fascist Italy. What the British Prime Minister, Chamberlain, had suspected Hitler had been up to when he had launched his peace offensive was now what Hitler suspected Roosevelt was up to in sending a peace envoy during the winter of 1940.

Division between the Axis partners was real. However, deeper *internal* divisions existed within the German government and war machine. Hitler's differences with Mussolini were potentially far less damaging than what was going on behind the scenes.

Coup d'État— for the Sake of Peace?

Two days after Warsaw's capitulation, Hitler ordered Army Commander-in-Chief General Walther von Brauchitsch and Army Chief of Staff General Franz Halder to begin preparations for an attack on France if an armistice was not forthcoming. Hitler thought that the Allies should be attacked in late fall, before the onset of winter, because time could only work against Germany's chances of winning the war. Hitler saw the principle of diminishing returns—the Allies could outproduce Germany in the long run.

The majority of the German general staff argued against going on the offensive in November 1939. They argued that preparations could not be completed on time and that the campaign would surely last through the winter months. Among those opposed to Hitler's proposal to take the war to the

Allies before winter were Generals Gerd von Rundstedt, Fedor von Bock, Ritter von Leeb, Walter von Reichenau, and countless others of lower rank.

On October 27, Hitler gathered the leaders of the Wehrmacht for a conference. At this meeting, he revealed his arguments for the commencement of offensive operations against the British and French and designated November 12 as launch day. Word of the planned attack and the date that Hitler set was leaked to the coordinator of a group of conspirators, who intended to depose Hitler and end the war by negotiations with Britain and France. The leader of this coup d'état was General Hans Oster.

By November 2, the conspirators had nearly completed their plan of action. They drew up a comprehensive list of government officials who were to be arrested and imprisoned. A rough draft of a new government was put together by this time as well, with Beck as the new head of state. They had even worked out the details of a public proclamation to be announced to the German people after the coup had been carried out. The basic line to be followed in the announcement was that the coup had been designed to save Europe from another world war and that Hitler was "ill and temporarily incapacitated." Beck was to head an interim government that would call for elections as soon as all internal disturbances caused by Nazi sympathizers had been brought under control.

The plan involved some adept trickery. Hitler was to be spirited away to safety by one group of conspirators on the false premise that the SS was conducting a coup against Hitler. They were to "secure" Hitler and pretend to take him to safety. Once Hitler had been removed to "safety," he would be arrested.

For this scheme to work, some of Germany's top generals had to take part. Although all of the leading generals were in agreement that Hitler's idea for a fall offensive would end in disaster, they were not convinced that betraying Hitler in the midst of war was the best idea. Many of them still believed that Hitler could be convinced to put the offensive off until spring. The higher-ups were worried that the Allies would militarily exploit the conditions created by a coup and the internal civil-war-like conditions that were sure to follow. Many who had initially agreed with Oster's plan were, by November 4, hedging and uncommitted.

Conspirators Theo Kordt and Oster met that same day and mulled over the skittish nature of the general whom they regarded as being essential to carrying off the plan—Franz. Kordt contended that Halder was not dependable and would fail them at the crucial moment, so Kordt volunteered to assassinate Hitler himself. Kordt intended to use *explosives* to accomplish the deed.

Kordt and Oster turned out to be right about Halder. On November 5, Halder and Brauchitsch met with Hitler once again in an attempt to get him to delay the launching of a western offensive. In the conversation that followed, Hitler's words to Brauchitsch seemed to indicate that Hitler was on to the conspiracy. Hitler vowed to "destroy the spirit of resistance in Zossen." Both conspirators took Hitler's expression as a thinly veiled threat and feared that SS intelligence operatives may have already uncovered the plot. Upon returning to his army headquarters office in Zossen, Halder immediately contacted the other conspirators and demanded that all evidence of the conspiracy be destroyed immediately.[122]

The events of November 9, 1939, are extremely important when considering the German government's official intransigence. The first development was Britain and France's official rejection of the most recent appeal by the Belgian and Dutch monarchs for an end to hostilities.[123] This, of course, spared the German government from rejecting the offer themselves.

Hitler. A Bomb. A Plan?

The second event of the day shocked the Nazi hierarchy to the core. A bomb had exploded, killing eight and injuring sixty, shortly after Hitler had left the Munich Bürgerbraukeller, where he had made a speech to some of the old Nazi Party comrades.

The bomb, intended to kill Hitler, did not go off in time. It exploded after the Führer had already left for Nuremberg by train.

When Hitler and his entourage learned of the incident—as their train had stopped in Nuremberg—the immediate reaction on the part of all present was that it had been "an assassination attempt" hatched in London.[124] After a quick staff meeting, it was decided to keep any allegations of British involvement under wraps until they "at least knew from where the attempt came."[125] It could have been an attempted coup d'état for all they knew at the time, and they did not want to tip off those involved, lest the culprits discover that they were on to them.

The next day the attempt was reported in Paris and London, along with accusations that the Nazis had committed another "Reichstag Fire."[126] Of course, that was a groundless accusation. There is not even the slightest evidence that it had been a propaganda stunt by the Nazis. It would make more sense that the afore-mentioned German conspirators were involved—especially considering that Kordt is on record planning to use explosives to pull off a coup d'état. Even though Chamberlain made it known at the time that it was his official desire that Hitler be thrown out of power, it remains simply a matter of interest that two days after the attempt on

Hitler's life Chamberlain wrote his sister of his desire to see Hitler dead or put into an insane asylum—for both options had been under consideration by the German conspirators. These conspirators did have contacts with British agents, but no solid connection has ever been established.[127]

The assassination attempt caused retrenchment among the belligerents and increased anxiety among the neutrals. Many expected that the war would start in earnest before the onset of winter. Indeed, as previously mentioned, Hitler wanted to attack France before winter because he perceived that Chamberlain's Peace Front strategy might just work. To a degree, it was working in the late fall of 1939.

The "Peace Front" at Work

By the end of November, it was clear that Chamberlain's Peace Front strategy was working on two levels. Internal division in Germany was obviously occurring, and the German and Italian economies were beginning to feel the far-reaching influence of British and French domination of international trade and commerce.

Prime Minister Chamberlain's leading economic advisors agreed with him that Germany could be brought to dire straits come the middle of winter if the economic "noose" could be tightened sufficiently. This tightening was aimed at shortening the war and *winning the peace*. Stage one of Chamberlain's plan involved the consolidation of British interests abroad, especially oil and merchant traffic directly connected to the German war economy. The second phase involved spreading out the war beyond Germany's logistical capabilities. It was also a way of decreasing Germany's ability to hit the western Allies directly with a concentrated and sustainable force. At the core of this strategy were two regions: Scandinavia and the Balkans. Allied interest in Norway's merchant fleet and Swedish iron ore, which played an important part in supplying the Ruhr with raw materials, is perhaps the best example of how phase one and two of Chamberlain's Peace Front strategy was to function.

In Chamberlain's plan, the German war machine could be severely damaged over the winter months, while the Allies could build up their military capabilities in France and secure the cooperation of Belgium and the Netherlands—who would naturally be drawn to the Allied side. Time looked to be on the side of the Allies in terms of production of war material and the ability to spread Germany thin by initiating other diversionary fronts. The overwhelming advantage that the Allies had on the high seas was the key to pulling the strategy off. Perhaps a boxing metaphor might be useful in understanding the situation. The Allies chose to fight Germany like Muhammad Ali fought Frazier—avoid head-to-head exchanges and close combat, force your opponent to change his game plan, stick and move, and make the enemy fight on unfamiliar ground.

One example of how the economic aspect of Chamberlain's strategy was working can be found in the case of Spain. Before the war, Spain and Germany carried on a thriving barter trade. This trade had been cut off by the Allied naval blockade of Europe, forcing Spain to seek a similar agreement with *France* for raw materials. So, here was Franco's Spain, who himself would not have been in power without German and Italian assistance, now compelled to trade with Hitler's enemies in order to avoid economic disaster.[128]

Another case in point was the Allies' influence in Romania. The Allies achieved control of Romania's oil refineries without firing a shot. Financial control of Romania's oil refineries was all that was necessary.[129]

The overall picture looked mighty bleak for Germany. Right off the bat, Germany lost 20% of some of its most essential imported raw materials because trade between the Allies and Germany had been brought to a halt. If the German economy were to keep its head above water over the winter, Germany would be forced to make up this loss by dramatically increasing their trade with nations such as Yugoslavia, Greece, Turkey, Spain and Sweden.[130] Of course, the Allies were already well on their way to making sweet trade deals with all of these nations. In most cases, unless these nations were intimidated by their close geographic position to Germany or Italy, they were easily bought off by the British and French.

By the end of November 1939, the British government had secured 2.2 million tons of Norway's tanker and merchant fleet. As represented by these figures and many more, it is obvious that the economic deals struck between Moscow and Berlin ended up being a crucial sustaining force for the German war economy over the winter months. Simply said, Soviet economic collaboration was the leading factor in foiling Chamberlain's Peace Front strategy, in economic terms. There can be no doubt that Stalin robbed the Allies of their economic advantage. The USSR retained its neutral status, but how can anyone refrain from placing a large portion of the blame *at their feet* for the stunning defeats the Allies were to face in the spring and summer of 1940? Could Germany have mustered such an overwhelming military campaign without a stable economy? The answer is obviously "no." So often Chamberlain and Daladier are blamed for the defeats that were to come—however, the Soviets deserve the lion's share of the credit.

Whereas the "neutral" Soviet actions over the winter months worked against Chamberlain's Peace Front strategy, the neutral United States was another matter altogether.[131] The US government's actions tended to support Chamberlain's strategy in the fall and winter months.

The Influence of Munich on FDR

In November of 1939, the Roosevelt administration retained a somewhat separate perspective on recent history, even though it is clear where the President's sympathies lay. Roosevelt was able to retain his freedom of action on the diplomatic front as a neutral, while often working covertly to prop up the Allied Peace Front strategy. Here, a brief review of US involvement is necessary.

Back in September of 1938, William Bullit, the US ambassador to France, had pleaded with Roosevelt to call on all of the European powers involved in the German-Czechoslovakian crisis over the Sudetenland, to meet in The Hague and work out a formula for a peaceful solution. President Roosevelt, at the time of this particular crisis, had decided to pursue a slightly different approach than Bullit recommended.

Despite US Secretary of State Cordell Hull's protestations, the President had called upon Undersecretary of State Sumner Welles and Assistant Secretary of State Adolf Berle to draw up an appeal to the President of Czechoslovakia, Eduard Benes, and the German chancellor, Adolf Hitler.[132] As events pushed along on the way to the now infamous Munich Conference, Roosevelt had found diplomatic leverage in attempting to develop a relationship with the Italian head of state, Benito Mussolini. Roosevelt followed a policy of placing diplomatic pressure on Germany through Italy; the official hope being to place Mussolini under the international microscope and thereby use the Duce to get key concessions out of Hitler during the German-Czechoslovakian crisis. To this end, Roosevelt's dealings with Mussolini had been a success. Mussolini stepped in on a number of occasions during the Munich Conference to take off the edge of Hitler's threats to use military force to end the crisis.[133]

Roosevelt had correctly surmised that Hitler would become extremely nervous about the prospect of war with Czechoslovakia, if faced with doubt of Italy's support. Since FDR found some leverage in 1938 with Mussolini, perhaps he could make a repeat performance in early 1940.

Even if there was little hope left that Roosevelt could orchestrate a climb-down by Germany by similar methods, the President felt that he could, at the very least, bolster the Allied cause by helping to divide the Axis partners.

Harkening back to Roosevelt's words from early 1939 is highly instructive in terms of coming to grips with what the US President was now up to in early 1940. On the very same day that FDR had made a public appeal to Hitler and Mussolini for peace (back on April 14, 1939), he also wrote to his Secretary of Agriculture, Henry Wallace. FDR wrote that "the two madmen respect force and force alone," and that "the most feasible way out is to use methods which would tend to drive a wedge between the two madmen."[134]

Is it a coincidence that at the onset of the war in September 1939, the idea of driving a wedge between Hitler and Mussolini had been included as a stage in Chamberlain's Peace Front strategy? Chamberlain and Daladier believed that it might be possible to separate Italy from Germany by a combination of economic and political pressure. This is hardly a coincidence, of course.[135]

The Italian Question

It seems likely that Roosevelt's attention to the Mussolini factor was again stirred by the Italian foreign minister's address to the Fascist Grand Council on December 16, 1939.

What was it in Ciano's address that got Roosevelt's fertile mind going? Here is a snippet from Ciano's speech:

We [in the Italian government] did not fail to let the Reich know the reasons why the Fascist Guard would have desired a peaceful solution, or at least a localization of the conflict.

To add teeth to his proclamation, Ciano made public that the Pact of Steel contained an unpublished proviso, in which both governments had pledged to do everything in their power to avoid a war in Europe for three years.[136]

Beyond this revelation, the Italian statesman went on to express his nation's deepest sympathies with the Finnish people in their struggle against Soviet aggression.

Roosevelt simply connected the dots, as the British government had when they heard how upset the Italian government had become with Hitler's dealings with the USSR. It seemed as if Hitler had betrayed his anti-communist principles for the perfidy of a temporary deal with the devil. Moreover, this betrayal on Hitler's part had led to Soviet encroachment all over eastern Europe. Now the brave people of Finland were under the Soviet gun—and the Nazi-Soviet pact seemed to be largely responsible for emboldening the USSR.

The "Winter War"

The Italian people were especially fond of the Finns, and how they were standing up to the "Soviet Colossus." Mussolini, with broad popular support, had committed the Italian government to sending aid to the Finns—especially military hardware. The same popular movement was taking form in Britain, France, and the United States. All of the governments of these nations were considering sending military aid, economic aid, and even volunteer units to fight in the Russo-Finnish war. The Germans, who had been long-time friends of Finland, were forced into official silence due to their desire to placate Stalin. Obviously, there was a crack in the relationship between Rome and Berlin. Perhaps this crack would be just the place to drive a wedge between Hitler and Mussolini.

On the surface, the Russo-Finnish war seemed like an unwelcome complication in the scheme of things, as far as the Allies were concerned. On the surface, it appeared to destroy Anglo-Soviet and Franco-Soviet relations. However, in keeping with the Chamberlain Peace Front strategy, the Allied leadership immediately recognized the possible value of this side show as a way of getting Germany to commit to a risky Scandinavian campaign. In short, the Allies could use the notion of "aid to Finland" as an excuse to bring all of Scandinavia under its wings. The possibility of switching the war to Scandinavia was a way of getting Germany to embark on an unsustainable, logistically straining, diversionary campaign.

The relationship between the Allies and Soviets had gone from bad to worse in the beginning of December 1939. The British and French led a successful effort to expel the USSR from the League of Nations.[137]

This expulsion should not be viewed in isolation of other previous events. The Allies were already thoroughly disgusted with Stalin prior to the Soviet invasion of Finland. They were upset with Stalin, first and foremost because he had made a pact with Hitler for the dismemberment of Poland. Beyond that, there was a rapid cooling of relations due to the fact that the Soviets publicly sided with Germany in calling for an end to the war between Germany, Britain and France over Poland.

Soviet Foreign Minister Molotov's speech to the Supreme Soviet of October 31 had sent a cold shiver down the spine of Allied statesmen at the time. Molotov outlined a new German-Soviet "rapprochement," insisting, "Germany's position is that of a state which is striving for the earliest termination of war and for peace," and scolding the Allies for their opposition "to the conclusion of peace." Molotov did not stop there. He went on to challenge the position of *moral integrity*, which the British and French were claiming as their primary reason for continuing the fight even after Poland was defeated. The foreign minister claimed that there was no justification for an "ideological war on Germany" by the Allies—citing what he called Allied "duplicity." He specifically singled out the British government's claim to be "fighting for democracy" for open derision—pointing out the "suppression of political liberties throughout its colonial empire."[138]

Nearly a month later, Stalin echoed Molotov's sentiments in an address in which he held the Allies responsible for the war and spoke bitterly of the rulers who had "rudely rejected both Germany's peace proposals and the Soviet Union's efforts to bring the war quickly to an end."[139]

To complicate matters, one day after Stalin's haranguing of the Allies the Soviets attacked Finland! This attack rekindled the fear among many Allied statesmen of a possible German-Soviet secret military agreement. However, to other Allied leaders, the Soviet attack on Finland indicated that the Nazis and Soviets could not possibly remain partners for long. These statesmen knew how distasteful it was for most Germans, especially Nazis, to stand by idly as Finland was bullied by Stalin. Germany, after all, had for years been on the closest terms with Finland. Allied leaders, Churchill in particular, prophesied that the new German-Soviet arrangement could not overcome so many years of intense suspicions, ideological differences, and plain hatred. Whatever newfangled diplomatic experiment existed between Nazi Germany and Soviet Russia was bound to come unraveled. It was the task of the British and French governments to facilitate this unraveling and somehow regain the USSR as an ally against Hitler. Therefore, when it came to the precarious Russo-Finnish War the Allies would have to take a "moral" stand against Stalin's aggression, but hold off on doing anything that might cause irreparable harm.

Similarly, but from a position a bit further removed, Roosevelt spoke of placing a "moral embargo" upon the Soviet Union for its actions against Finland. A peculiar three-way connection existed—Chamberlain's Peace Front strategy, the Italian Question, and the Finnish question were connected at the hip, as far as the President was concerned, to the possibility of making inroads with Mussolini in the hopes of detaching him from Hitler. Recalling, once again, the Italian foreign minister's speech of December 16, 1939, there was a confluence of events that was just irresistible for the American President. When the time was ripe, Roosevelt would send Sumner Welles on his famous peace mission.

The German Government's Take on the War Within the War

From the Hitler-Ribbentrop perspective, the worsening of Anglo-Soviet–Franco-Soviet relations was a relief. The Soviet government's suspicion that the Allies had only ever intended to use the USSR as a "shock absorber" seemed reconfirmed with the Soviet expulsion from the League of Nations. Hitler and Ribbentrop felt justified in their long-standing contention that the only reason for the USSR's admittance to the League of Nations in the first place had been to better fulfill their obligation to the Franco-Soviet Alliance. Ribbentrop never failed to poke his Soviet counterpart with the perception that once the geopolitical "encirclement of Germany" had been obliterated, the western Allies' need for the Soviet Union had also vanished. Moreover, in some respects, the war with Finland had become a positive development for Germany.

No matter which side was winning at any given moment, the Allies' "moral" stand would continue to strain Allied-Soviet relations. It was in the interest of the Hitler-Ribbentrop policy for the Winter War to drag on and for the Finns to hold their ground. Perhaps the Allies would continue to send economic and material aid to Finland. Even better, maybe they would do something foolhardy—like sending troops!

All of these possibilities would tend to put the kybosh on any Allied-Soviet rapprochement. In fact, the best-case scenario, as far as the Nazi regime was concerned, would have been for the Soviets to suffer damaging blows at the hands of an Allies-supported Finnish army.[140] Since the German government was secretly supplying the Finns with intelligence and military expertise, one can only imagine what confusion would have ensued.[141]

The Allies Look North to Avoid a "Head-On"

On the other hand, regardless of what Churchill claimed later on, it was in the interest of the Allies to end the Finnish war on a positive note *for the Soviet Union*. This opinion was not uniformly held among the Allied leadership, but it was Churchill who was *the most eager* to see the Winter War end on a positive note for the Soviets.[142]

Churchill would like the reader of his memoirs to believe that the planned Allied expedition to capture Norwegian and Swedish iron ore, to seize Trondheim, Stravanger and other key Norwegian fjord-ports, was somehow necessarily tied to the armed support of the Finns. This is only partially true. If one compares Paul Reynaud's[143] version of the same story, one cannot help but recognize that the Finnish War was viewed by many members of the Allied Supreme War Council as a major *obstacle*. Many felt that it was not safe to gamble on the possibility of war with the Soviets, even if the plan had been to stop short of actually helping the Finns, because the Allies felt they could count on German countermeasures.[144] In other words, they were counting on making Scandinavia a theater of operations, knowing that Germany would respond militarily.

Some drastic notions were floated at some of these meetings of the Allied Supreme War Council. Like the bombing of Soviet oil fields in the Caucasus, or the opening of a new front in the Balkans. As the winter dragged on without any significant ratcheting up of hostilities between the western Allies and Germany, the Allied War Cabinets decided that the time had come to go to stage two of the Chamberlain Peace Front strategy—spreading the war out. According to Paul Reynaud's memoirs, "In Gamelin's opinion, the problem was one of making Germany fight; of forcing her both to take the offensive on our own front and to open new theatres of operations."[145]

Confirmation of Paul Reynaud's memoirs is found in two other sources. The French foreign minister, Georges Bonnet, wrote that Gamelin wanted to force Hitler "to precipitate things and invade Holland and Belgium."[146]

The Ironsides Diaries provides an even more detailed confirmation. Ironsides provides the following glimpse into the Allied command strategy:

1. Keep Germany looking north and force her to divert key forces from the western front.

2. Churchill thought that the occupation of Narvik etc. should go forward "without the pretext of helping the Finns."

3. Reynaud and Gamelin pushed for active intervention in Scandinavia.

4. Gamelin hoped that the Germans would attack.

5. He [Ironsides] personally believed that Hitler would want "to push for a patched-up peace at any moment."[147]

Lest the reader be left under the mistaken impression that the Allied thinking was something new, the fact is that just six days after the aforementioned Ciano speech, which had exposed a division among the Axis partners, the British War Cabinet met and discussed at length how they "might go further and switch the war into Scandinavia."[148]

Winston Churchill put it this way during the November 16, 1939, meeting of the British War Cabinet:

> No doubt it appears reasonable to the Soviet Union to take advantage of the present situation.... This applies not only to Baltic territories, but also to Finland. It is in our interest that the USSR should increase their strength in the Baltic...it would be a mistake for us to stiffen the Finns against making concessions to the USSR.

And

> I think it would be to our advantage if the trend of events in Scandinavia brought it about in Norway and Sweden were forced into the war...we would then be able to gain a foothold in Scandinavia... without having to go to the extent of ourselves declaring war on Russia.[149]

The evidence is overwhelming. The Allies were moving closer and closer to initiating the next stage of Chamberlain's strategy by spreading the war out.

The notion of starting another front seems to have been originally a French suggestion, which was supported by Churchill and Hore-Belisha as long as war with the Soviets could be avoided. The French government wanted to avoid a First World War scenario. Fighting another head-on war with Germany was not an attractive prospect. Avoiding a war on French soil was their primary concern. So, the notion of switching the war to another theater of operations was perfectly sensible from a French point of view. Late in the Great War—World War I—a little-written-about Allied military adventure designed to cut off Germany's supplies of iron ore from Scandinavia had played a crucial role in crippling the German economy and provoking internal strife in Kaiser Wilhelm's Germany.[150] The Allied war planners were not about to wait four years—this time around—before taking action on this front. They theorized that nearly four years of unbelievable bloodshed might have been avoided, had the Allies switched the war to Scandinavia in 1914!

The Italian Question's Connection to Scandinavia

A more subtle reason for the Allied plan to switch the war to Scandinavia was the curious "Italian Question." As long as the leading Allied statesmen believed that they had a diplomatic shot at driving a wedge between the Axis nations, Chamberlain's Peace Front policy could avoid radical revision by its internal critics.

Churchill, Gamelin, and Reynaud were all formally "on board" in their support of Chamberlain's plan. These revisionists were always attempting to push things along *ahead of schedule*. They typically desired to *combine* stages. They had little patience with a plan that seemed to be taking so long to fully develop. The pressure exerted on Chamberlain in Britain and Daladier in France to alter the plan was enormous and continuous. The only point of complete agreement between the Chamberlain crowd and the Churchill crowd was the "Italian Factor." Therefore, the Italian Factor was the glue, which held Chamberlain's Peace Front strategy together. Chamberlain was pressured to skip ahead in his scheme by spreading the war to the Balkans, the Middle East, and to North Africa. Many of these, like the Churchill-inspired plan to start up a Balkan front as soon as possible, were looked upon with open ridicule by Chamberlain and his clique.

Alexander Cadogan, a member of that clique, refers in his diaries to the internal squabble within the British government over how best to prosecute the war and how to best "win the peace." One can see that the debate concerning the Scandinavian and Balkan schemes were *both* viewed in the *common context* of the Italian Question. The notion remained that Italy could be separated from Germany. For instance, Cadogan reports that he had talked the situation over with Lord Halifax, and that both had come to the conclusion that they should "go easy on that" [the Balkan scheme] until the Mussolini question was definitely resolved in the negative.[151] It is intriguing to note Mussolini's mood at the time of this Cadogan-Halifax conversation.

Italian Foreign Minister Galaezzo Ciano relates in his diary entry of December 26, 1939, that the Duce wanted a German defeat! Even if this was an exaggeration on Ciano's part, Cadogan, Halifax and others must have been on to something.

On December 27, the British War Cabinet discussed the question of a new diplomatic approach to Italy. At the meeting, it is revealed that the French ambassador to Italy had beaten them to the punch. The French government had already begun to work on Mussolini.[152] The French ambassador, Francois-Poncet, had initiated the contact.

The Allies had been working on the diplomatic front in an attempt to create a "Balkan Bloc" to check further Nazi-Soviet meddling in the region and to keep these nations from becoming attached to Germany by way of alliance. In this connection, the Allied governments wanted to bring to the surface the divergent interests of Italy and Germany in the Balkans, in the hopes of separating the two Axis partners. The Italian diplomatic documents from this time make it clear that the French had been working to whet Mussolini's interest in the Balkans since the last week of September 1939.[153]

To ease tensions between Britain and Italy, the British government had decided to mollify its stand on the question of Italian trade and shipping. In a classic example of Chamberlain's Peace Front policy, Italy's economic needs were to be exploited to lay the groundwork for a political understanding with Italy.

Much of the trade question between the Allies and Italy involved the free flow of coal from Northern Europe to Italy. On March 9, 1940, Ralph Stevenson, the principal private secretary to the British State Secretary, had returned from Rome with good news for Mr. Chamberlain. Alexander Cadogan relates that it...

> Looks as if we'd settled the coal question. A smack in the eye of Ribbentrop on his arrival in Rome, when I expect that he hoped to rope the Italians into the war. There may be something in "appeasement" yet![154]

Here we see a direct connection, in Cadogan's mind, between "appeasement" and Chamberlain's Peace Front policy.

Yet another strange confirmation of what the Allies were up to comes from an American source. Assistant Secretary of State Berle felt that he had to make an official protest to the British government concerning the holding up of US ships at Gibraltar. He wrote the following in his diary as a summary of the events:

They do this in order to make it hard for our ships and at the same time make it easy for the Italian ships, so that the Italians can feel they have discriminatory treatment.[155]

The Pope's Call for Peace

An approach to Italy invariably involved the Catholic Church. Pope Pius XII's Christmas speech had outlined his belief that the guarantees of security were the prerequisites for a peaceful solution. The Pope had also made a curious reference in his address to the brave soldiers of Finland. The Pope's Christmas Eve address was given in front of the College of Cardinals. In the speech, he outlined "Five Postulates for Peace."

These postulates included:

1. Independence of all nations guaranteed.
2. The freedom from the slavery of armaments.
3. The reconstruction of international institutions.
4. The granting of fair demands for minority populations living under foreign rule.
5. That the leaders of all nations must observe international pacts faithfully.[156]

Prior to this speech President Roosevelt had sent a letter to Pope Pius XVI. FDR's letter was sent on December 23, 1939, informing the Holy See of his decision to send Myron C. Taylor as a special US envoy. The letter also made a positive reference to the Pope's recent discussions with the king of Italy and Mussolini, in which all three leaders had agreed that a peaceful solution to the European conflict should be found.

After the Pope's Christmas Eve address, FDR once again sent a letter to the Holy See. This time Roosevelt was more cautious in his wording. He did not want the Pope to be left under the impression that he, Roosevelt, wanted to serve as a broker of peace. The letter was crafted to avoid being drawn into a move for peace, while, at the same time, not seeming to entirely repudiate the Pope's efforts. Roosevelt put it succinctly:

> In these present moments no spiritual leader, no civic leader, can move forward on a specific plan to terminate destruction and build anew.[157]

The writer of a *Newsweek* article covering the announcement of Myron C. Taylor's appointment as a special envoy to the Holy See summed up the President's reasoning with incredible accuracy:

> The British and French, believing they have the Germans and Russians on the run, do not want peace now. The President shares their anxiety

lest Berlin and Moscow seize upon such an appeal as the Pope's to extricate themselves from a difficult situation, hence does not wish to do Britain and France the disservice of appearing to endorse a plea for immediate peace. Yet he wishes to leave the door always open for a peace offensive in which he might play a major role.[158]

FDR was sending a special envoy to the Holy See in order to better tap into the back channel communications on the situation. He believed the development of closer diplomatic relations with the Vatican would open up more avenues of communication—avenues on both sides of the conflict. The President wanted to gain the most accurate picture possible before the expected spring offensives. In short, the President was doing what was prudent—no matter who came out on top after the real shooting started, his position would be more secure and he could have all the available diplomatic channels at his disposal for *when the time was ripe for a lasting peace.*

Prelude to a Peace Mission

January 3 and 4 were significant days in the maintenance of the German mood of intransigence. On both days more rumors of peace, emanating from the "Vatican and neutral powers" came to the attention of the German Foreign Office and Propaganda Ministry. These leads were considered by the German government to be a sly ploy to undermine the German will to war. At the same time, the news regarding Germany's position among the surrounding nations was equally disturbing.

On January 4, 1940, intelligence reports indicated that the Romanian government was feeling dangerously "pro-Entente." In addition, the Hungarian government was demanding Germany's diplomatic assistance in squeezing territorial concessions out of its neighbors. The Hungarian request even included a thinly veiled threat—these territorial concessions were required in return for its "non-participation in the war."[159]

The very idea that Hungary and Romania might join forces with the Allies must have been disconcerting to the German government.

Most important, though, was Mussolini's personal letter to Hitler. It was filled with the sort of language that could have occurred in Hitler and Ribbentrop's worst nightmares. In the letter, the Duce intimated that Hitler should have come to an understanding with the Allies, before going to war with Poland. Mussolini repeated his willingness to act as a mediator.[160]

Mussolini was angered with Hitler because he felt that the German government had *sacrificed its principles* to the "tactical exigencies" of the moment. To clarify this point, the Italian dictator added that he considered it his *duty* to warn Hitler that *any further warming in German-Soviet relations* would result in "catastrophic repercussions in Italy."

Mussolini did not stop there with his critical insights. He specifically reprimanded Ribbentrop for not having believed—before the outbreak of the Polish war—that the Allies would declare war.[161] What else could Hitler do at this point other than hold the current line with the Soviets and hope that they refrained from making any moves in eastern Europe, until Hitler had moved to assure the Duce that this relationship was really just a sham. Stalin had really put Hitler in a bind.[162]

Is it a coincidence, considering the Duce's attitude in January of 1940 that the Allies were thinking in terms of coming to an understanding with Fascist Italy? It was no coincidence.

Roosevelt Waits in the Wings

Across the Atlantic, President Roosevelt remained free from the specific trapping of Allied intransigence, even if his sympathies were clearly not neutral. Even if the President's actions seem to have worked hand in glove with Chamberlain's Peace Front strategy, the American President retained his diplomatic freedom of action. Roosevelt was not encumbered by the official intransigence of nations jockeying for the best position in a coming bloodbath. Rather, he was free to jockey for a better position to act as a mediator for peace, *when the proper time came.* It is tempting to conclude that the President was only seriously considering acting as a broker for peace with a *broken Germany* and a *victorious France and Britain.* However, the President was astute enough to know that *nothing was certain* once the war really got under way. He was capable of imagining a few scenarios, short of an outright Allied victory, where his services might come in handy—especially if the war bogged down in World War I fashion. The President's Assistant Secretary of State's diary of December 29, 1939, provides a glimpse into what might have been on the President's mind when he sent Welles to Rome, Berlin, Paris and London, to investigate the prospects for a peaceful solution:

> My private opinion is that the President's mind is working towards trying to summon a general peace conference before the beginning of the spring drives. I agree that this will not be ideal. But I do not see that it will be any more ideal, no matter who comes out top dog in the spring and summer fighting.[163]

FDR felt that the Welles mission was his responsibility—especially considering that he believed that the US might very well eventually be drawn into the war. During the German-Czechoslovakian crisis of 1938, Roosevelt had told Cordell Hull, "It's safe to urge peace until the last moment."[164] Nothing had altered the President's view in 1939. He still held to essentially the same position in the winter and early spring of 1940.

On the other hand, there was *one* significant difference in FDR's position in January of 1940. Because of the Munich experience, the President had taken on the perspective that "security" was the paramount issue in the establishment of a "just" and "long-term" peace. The appeasement of Hitler during the Sudetenland crisis had brought the President in line with the Allied version of what was necessary for a "just" and "long-term" peace. Giving in to Hitler's version of an ethnographically "just" solution to that problem had led to the further collapse of what had been Czechoslovakia, and that nation's military occupation by Hitler's Wehrmacht. Roosevelt saw the same ethnographically "just" Hitlerian demands on Poland lead down the path to war as well.

The Great Divide

On the other side of this great divide, the German and Italian governments formed their concept of a "just" peace upon the following criteria:

1. Solve the nationalities problem by reconstructing states by the use of strict, racial-cultural criteria. This belief was founded in the experiences of the start of the First World War. In Hitler's mind or Mussolini's mind, it had been the existence of multi-ethnic, multi-cultural, European states that was the powder keg of the Great War—the "crazy multi-national quilt" of the Austro-Hungarian Empire was most often used by them as an example of the root cause of war in Europe. If national boundaries could be redrawn to correspond with ethnic and cultural distinctions, war was much less likely to break out. Both Nazism's and Fascism's definition of nation state were racist.

2. The British and French governments had no right to meddle in the affairs of eastern Europe. It is seldom pointed out by historians in their appraisal of the Rome-Berlin Axis that this alliance was not just vertical, but horizontal. Hitler and Mussolini had established the concept of a "Horizontal Axis." Draw a line in an eastward fashion from the Austrian-Italian border and one can get the basic idea of their shared vision of each nation's sphere of influence in eastern Europe. This horizontal axis was in keeping with Hitler's vision of a future eastern-European "Lebensraum," as well as satisfying Mussolini's future vision of an Italian-dominated Balkans—which was the key in his mind to the resurrection of Rome's past glories.

These two dictators were ultimately partners because their visions of the future were complementary. Hitler wished this had been true in his relationship to Britain, but, of course, it was not.[165]

In the beginning of February 1940, Hitler still held on to a *powerful delusion*. The delusion that he might be able to come to an understanding with Britain and end the war in the west. Hitler's *racism* is what sustained this persistent pipe dream. The idea of a "natural kinship" with the British people never allowed his narrow mind to escape it either—even after his vision of the future had been rejected repeatedly. Yes, the German warlord was planning to attack the Allies. However, in his mind, pulverizing them seemed to be the only way to *force them to come to the peace table*. Therefore, it should not be surprising to find that Hitler still privately hankered after peace, even in the winter and spring months of 1940.

Evidence of this desire on Hitler's part can be found in the memoirs of Felix Kersten. Kersten had an in-depth conversation with Heinrich Himmler, the Chief of the SS, on February 6, 1940. In this conversation, Himmler informed Kersten of the details of a recent meeting with Hitler. Here is what Kersten recalls:

> He [Himmler] told me that the Führer had had very welcome news about the position in England. The people there did not want a war and everything pointed to the fact that England would soon be putting out peace feelers, which would certainly not be rejected but welcomed as an expression of Greater German solidarity....[166]

Himmler went on to tell Kersten of his own personal views as to why peace was still possible. Himmler, just like Hitler, said that ultimately the two nations would come to an understanding based on their *racial brotherhood*. The notorious head of the SS then quoted Hitler as saying that he "would be magnanimous in his treatment of England."[167]

The depths of the Nazi fantasy world surfaced again in yet another conversation between Kersten and Himmler. This time, the Reichsführer SS predicted that the king of England would one day receive Hitler in London, and that the two would sit down as equal partners to "conclude a just peace to protect the Germanic race throughout the world."[168]

Enter Sumner Welles

It was "In the first days of January, 1940, that [according to Welles] the President sent for me."[169] The Undersecretary of State had been called to the Oval Office by Roosevelt, who had decided to use Welles again as he once had in 1938, during the German-Czechoslovakian crisis over the Sudetenland. Welles would visit Rome, Berlin, Paris, and London—and in that order. What had brought the President to this decision was the aforementioned "Italian Question." The division between Hitler and Mussolini beckoned.

The German foreign minister, Ribbentrop, had finally had enough of the Italian ambassador to Berlin, Attalico. Ribbentrop contacted the Italian foreign minister, Ciano, and demanded his *immediate recall*. Why was Ribbentrop so steamed? Because Attalico had not only announced his desire for peace publicly, but also had been using what amounted to the Allied version of what a "just" peace would entail.

In fact, in late January, the American ambassador in Rome, Phillips, sent two secret telegrams "for Welles" which indicated that it may have been Attalico's recall that had first caught FDR's imagination. Phillips' telegram further refers to the President's hope "that the Italian government would continue to remain neutral."[170]

On February 1, Roosevelt explained his reasoning behind the Welles mission to the British ambassador to the US, Lord Lothian. Roosevelt told the British ambassador that his concept of a "just" peace was identical to that of His Majesty's Government: including the restoration of freedom for the Czechs and Poles; solid assurances against renewed aggression; and the establishment of the ubiquitous "four freedoms."[171] This statement stands as testimony that Roosevelt sent Welles to work on the same project that the Allied governments had been focusing on since the discovery of strained German-Italian relations.

The publicly stated reason for the Welles mission was to find out what the views of the "four governments" were and to ascertain whether there were any "possibilities of concluding any just and permanent peace." Roosevelt felt that no solution of this sort was likely and was aware that "Mr. Chamberlain himself had long ago decided that there was no hope for British security."[172] Still, something about the idea of using Italy as a diplomatic lever seemed to have the faint hint of possibilities. The Italian Question, without a doubt, was at the center of Welles' mission. Welles quotes the President as saying:

> Only in Italy was it remotely conceivable that the policy of this government might have some concrete effect. If by some means the United States could prevent Italy from actually taking part in the war against France and Great Britain, if Hitler could not obtain the active participation of his southern partner in the attack on France, the outcome of the war might be less certain than it then seemed.[173]

The period between Roosevelt's decision to call upon Welles in "the first days of January" and February 9, when the mission was made public, is crucial in understanding the mission's interplay with Allied intransigence and strategy. In the first two months of 1940, Allied plans were beginning to congeal. The Allied Supreme War Council had worked out the initial draft of a planned offensive of their own against Nazi Germany.[174] To those less informed of the President's intentions, Roosevelt seemed to be throwing a wrench into the works. After all, Allied war planners were on the brink of getting the war machine into gear in Scandinavia. Many saw the Welles mission as a downer to Allied soldierly morale as well. Roosevelt's peculiar posturing was disconcerting to those Allied statesmen who were unaware of FDR's reasons. It was time for the daring deeds required in the next stage of Chamberlain's Peace Front strategy, not time for more talk.

The Welles Scare

The push to open up "a new front of attrition" against Germany by "opening a theater of operations in Scandinavia" was well under way.[175] The Allied war planners hoped to use Scandinavia to divert as much of Germany's strength as possible away from the western front.

British Admiral Ironsides was an integral part of the planning for this venture. He relates the following in his diaries:

> The German Army is now concentrated in great strength in a central position, making it extremely difficult to attack. Every large detachment which can be introduced will assist us when the time comes to make our decision to attack, without which the war is unlikely to end.[176]

And on January 25, 1940,

> The Gälivare [Sweden] project presents the first chance of upsetting the German's plans and making him disperse—An advance by us in Scandinavia, if it can be brought to pass, will create a great diversion of German force at small cost, [and] prevent Germany from carrying out her preconceived plan and cause her to improvise....[177]

And on February 15, 1940,

> ...we have worked out our plans in very great detail and I am sure that we can do the landing....The first troops sail on the 15th, under a month from now.[178]

On the French side of the plan, General Gustav-Maurice Gamelin's memorandum of March 16, 1940, goes into even greater detail:

We should forbid Sweden, under pains of blockade to sell her ore to Germany. If Sweden agrees, we will have gained our objective. If Germany should invade Sweden we will also have gained our objective, provided that we intervene before the spring thaw. If Sweden refuses, we should intercept Scandinavia's maritime trade, allowing us to negotiate for a commercial agreement which will strengthen our blockade.[179]

From another French source is yet another confirmation of what was being planned. Admiral Darlan, the commander of the French fleet, wrote:

It would be foolhardy to suppose that the Germans will take no action to counter our intervention in Norwegian waters. Germany has one vital preoccupation in her relations with Scandinavia, her iron ore imports....It is not unreasonable to imagine that Germany will react to our diplomatic announcement or to our laying of mines [in Norwegian territorial waters]—that is, between April 3–6, invading Scandinavia to open up land communications with the sources of ore. If we do not wish to lose the initiative we must be ready to land forces in Norway—at Narvik in particular—to occupy the iron ore region before the Germans.[180]

Of course, no set of quotes of this sort would be complete without a Winston Churchill comment:

If they [the Germans] did invade Norway, I would be glad. They would become involved in a serious commitment."[181]

Churchill said this at a meeting of the British Admiralty, on January 3, 1940.

With such plans in the wings it is no wonder why many Allied statesmen reacted with horror at the potential of Welles' mission. So, why was Welles being sent by Roosevelt *now* that the Allies were finally geared up to take the war to the Germans?

Another Offer for a Patched-Up Peace?

On January 22, 1940, British Foreign Minister Lord Halifax and Alexander Cadogan perceived that the recent crescendo of peace rumors were "leading up to a last peace offensive" by the Germans. Two days later the same two men were feeling uneasy about the possibility of "a peace offensive in which we may find Roosevelt and the Pope associated" in the near future. This development caused some scrambling and brainstorming among the British and French leaders. The object was to come up with "an alternative" in the case that Britain would be put in the awkward position of turning down a call for peace that might be perceived as too sensible.[182] With the recent announcement from Berlin that Hitler was going to make another important address to the world on January 30, they were worried that the speech would be *another* appeal for peace. One can sense the relief felt by Cadogan in his diary entry on the day of the expected peace offensive—"Quite harmless…no peace offer. Thank God!"[183] The last thing the Allies wanted was for the US government to attach itself to another call for a patched-up peace!

A Matter of *Timing*

Roosevelt was on the same page as the Allies already, even though many did not know it. He did not want a patched-up peace either. The President had reconfirmed his position to Lord Lothian, the British ambassador to the US, a full week before the official announcement of the Welles mission on February 9, 1940.[184] Nevertheless, British and French newspapers were filled with scathing criticisms of Roosevelt's "untimely" and "undermining" diplomacy.

On the other hand, when one looks at the clarifying effect of the mission's announcement, one cannot help but notice that it helped to bring the newspaper editorials more into line with the real Allied objectives. In turn, public pressure had its effect on the average politician in Britain and France. For example, after the announcement of the Welles mission, the French Chambre des Députés, *without a single dissenting vote*, resolved to back up Premier Daladier's proclamation that the Allies must fight until a total Allied military victory was in hand.

The announcement of the Welles mission in the Allied press seems to have actually served as a *rallying point*. It served as a catalyst, arousing the private sector to talk, out in the open, about war aims and peace aims. The Welles mission seems to have reinvigorated, refocused and sharpened the definition of the Allies' will to war and the sort of peace they envisioned for the future of Europe.

Although one can find endless complaints in the diaries and memoirs of Allied leaders who were not directly involved with Welles, there is a curious absence of similar criticism on the part of those with whom Welles actually conferred. As previously stated, Lord Halifax had some prior knowledge of a peace offensive which would include Roosevelt. It is also obvious that Halifax did not have a very clear notion of what Roosevelt was intending. So, the questions remain, why did FDR wait until February to announce the mission, and when did he give those in the know a heads up?

The answer can be found in the chronological difference between US Secretary of State Cordell Hull's introduction of Roosevelt's plan to send Welles and Welles' own version. Hull has the idea for the mission hatched "Early in February," whereas Welles begins his version "early in January."[185]

One cannot fully understand the *timing* of Roosevelt's announcement of the mission until it is realized that according to the official British version, it was on *February 7, 1940*, that Chamberlain told Roosevelt of the Allied design to "aid" Finland through Norway and Sweden.[186] Furthermore, the French Premier, Daladier, seemed to be gearing up for something ominous. On the ninth of the month, Daladier's long-suffering struggle with the French Communists in Parliament came to an end. Breaking France's Constitutional protocol, *all* of the Communist deputies were *expelled*![187] It is also not a coincidence that on February 2, the Allied Supreme Council made its first definite decision to set a date for the Scandinavian campaign.[188] Roosevelt had actually known of the Allied scheme in "early January."[189] At that time the Allied plans for "switching the war to Scandinavia" were still developing. The difference between the Welles and Hull accounts is representative of Roosevelt's developing sense of urgency in the prosecution of a foreign policy idea that was rapidly running out of time.[190]

Roosevelt saw the Finnish and Soviet questions as inseparable. The place of Italy in Roosevelt's decision to send Welles in late February is also clear. In the beginning of January the Finnish foreign minister, Tanner, had attempted to enlist the Italian government in an attempt to end the Russo-Finnish Winter War. Tanner had suggested to the American minister in Helsinki, on January 9, that Italy and the US could be used to pressure Berlin into supporting the venture as well.[191]

Moscow: Not on *My* Itinerary

Another pertinent question regarding the Welles mission involves his mission's itinerary. If Rome, Berlin, Paris, and London, why not Moscow? If the intention of the Welles mission to visit these particular capitals was to find out "the present possibilities of concluding any just and permanent peace," then why not visit Moscow? The Soviets held a significant puzzle piece to the future security of Europe. How could FDR have imagined otherwise? Even if western military estimates did not accord the Soviets such a prominent place in the future of Europe, who was to say that Romania or Bulgaria did not face Poland's fate due to yet another Nazi-Soviet secret agreement? Although Roosevelt's reasoning on the matter of excluding Moscow is difficult to discern, *Welles'* reasons seem clear.

Sumner Welles had been the most outspoken member of the administration in the first weeks of December 1939, when the Soviets had attacked Finland. He had publicly endorsed a proposal to break off diplomatic relations with the USSR. In fact, a Welles-inspired bill had been introduced to Congress on February 7, 1940, calling for breaking of all diplomatic relations with the Soviets. This proposal was defeated by a three-vote margin in the House.[192]

US Assistant Secretary of State Adolf Berle noted Welles' attitude back on December 5, 1939, writing in his diary:

> Sumner is heavily for breaking relations with the Soviet Russians; the Secretary [Hull], more cautious is not; and I think the President agrees with him.[193]

Leaving Moscow off of the itinerary makes sense on another level as well—as a way of taking into account *Italian* sensibilities. Yes, this brings one back to the aforementioned Italian Factor as the leading reason for the mission. Welles had to demonstrate an obvious deference to the Italians, for any effort to detach Italy from its German ally to have any chance.[194]

Still another reason for Roosevelt's statement that "a visit to Moscow" would not "serve any useful purpose," was all wrapped up in Britain's recent diplomatic moves toward the Soviets. A British special envoy arrived in Moscow on the specific mission of bringing about a "rapprochement." The special envoy, Sir Stafford Cripps, reached Moscow on February 14, only three days before Welles opened up his talks with the Italian foreign minister, Galaezzo Ciano, at his office on the Palazzo Venezia in Rome.[195]

The final reason, and not an insignificant one at that, was Soviet economic collaboration with Nazi Germany. Soviet collaboration militated against Chamberlain's Peace Front policy. Therefore, a visit by Welles to Moscow may have seemed to legitimize Soviet foreign policy. In the weeks prior to Welles' arrival in Rome, the Germans and Soviets had signed *another* trade agreement. This agreement involved the Soviet's shipment of raw materials—particularly oil and foodstuffs—to Germany in return for German-manufactured products, including the latest in German arms technologies.[196]

On to Rome

Sumner Welles was received by the Italian foreign minister upon his arrival in Rome. Ciano and Welles had a brief introductory conversation. Ciano assured Welles that Hitler had genuinely desired to come to terms with the Allies in October of 1939. The Italian foreign minister went on to relate that the German government's attitude had significantly hardened over the winter months. He doubted that Hitler would even consider coming to terms with the

Allies any longer. After this short parley, Welles was ushered into the presence of the Duce.

At this historic meeting, Welles presented Mussolini with a personal letter from FDR. It was a message "of outstanding importance" emphasizing the US President's "desire for a continuation of Italian neutrality." The letter expressed Roosevelt's "emphatic desire to meet personally with the chief of the Italian government."[197] In Welles' memoir, *The Time for Decision,* he draws the reader aside and confides that:

> I am as confident today [1944, when he wrote it] as I was then [February 17, 1940] that he [Roosevelt] was right...that if he and Mussolini could meet in some relatively remote spot, such as the Azores, he could very probably persuade Mussolini that the best interest of Italy could be served if he refused to prostitute the Italian people to the greater glory of Hitler.[198]

After Mussolini had finished the letter, Welles set out the one proposal that he was empowered by Roosevelt to convey to the Duce.[199] Roosevelt proposed a far-reaching economic agreement intended for the betterment of relations between these two neutral states.

In the conversation following the proposal, the language of the two statesmen shifted rather rapidly from economics to geo-politics and the question of what Mussolini felt was the necessary basis for the realization of a long-term, peaceful solution to Europe's current problems. The divergent notions of a "just" future peace came to the fore.

Although Mussolini related his continuing belief in the possibility of a peaceful solution, he went on to clarify what he held to be the "just" basis upon which such a peace could be achieved and sustained. Mussolini targeted the nationalities question as being the primary incendiary for the present conflagration. For instance, he stated that he would support the re-emergence of a Polish state. However, he qualified this statement by declaring, "Poland should not again become a crazy quilt of diverse nationalities." The Duce remarked, "The poison of Europe during the past twenty years has been the question of minorities."[200] At this point in the meeting, Mussolini harkened back to the "injustice" of the Versailles system and expressed "utmost bitterness" against the British, because he felt that they had failed to understand the inherent geo-political instabilities created by the infamous treaty—especially in central and eastern Europe. In the end, Mussolini said that the geo-political questions must be solved *first.* Only after this issue had been addressed could any "guarantees of security" become a realistic goal.

Before the meeting came to a close, Welles asked one final question—was a negotiated peace still possible? To this question, Mussolini replied with an "emphatic yes." Welles felt that this response, alone, merited an unscheduled return to Rome at the end of his mission.

Berlin's Official Intransigence and Suspect Welles

Berlin was next on Sumner Welles' itinerary. At the time, the German government was doing its utmost to censor all information regarding Welles' presence. Ribbentrop was the source of this hush-hush effort. He had issued a directive calling upon all those involved in conversations with Welles to avoid talk of peace.[201] The reasoning behind this specific instance of German intransigence can be found in Hitler's current mindset. He was still reeling from the abrupt rejection of his call for peace back in October of 1939. Officially, Hitler wanted all who encountered Welles to "avoid showing any signs of readiness to compromise," because the Allies would only interpret this as "a sign of weakness" within his regime.[202]

Another indication of the German position of intransigence has been delineated by Erich Kordt, a member of Ribbentrop's advisory cabinet at the Foreign Ministry. In Kordt's book, *Wahn und Wirklichkeit* (Delusion and Reality), he writes that the German Foreign Ministry wanted to avoid kindling any "premature" or "illusionary" hopes of peace among the German people. Kordt also relates that there was a great deal of anxiety regarding Welles' visit to Rome. They were running scared on the possibility that Welles' mission might embolden the anti-German elements in Italy and, in turn, destroy the Rome-Berlin Axis.[203] This apprehension was well founded, considering FDR's reason for sending Welles in the first place.

An additional reason for the German attitude was the well-established intelligence that the Allies were in the final stages of their plan to carry out the "switching of the war to Scandinavia." Intelligence reports had been brought to Hitler's attention by Admiral Raeder in early December of 1939. As the fighting in Finland was drawing to a close, General Falkenhorst had been selected by the German army high command to develop a plan for a preemptive strike on Norway. The plan was preemptive in the sense that it was intended to deny the Allies their objectives. Since the German High Command was convinced that the Allies would act as soon as possible after the end of the Russo-Finnish war, there was a suspicion that the Welles mission was timed to *distract* Hitler.[204] The Russo-Finnish War had ended only days before Welles departed for Europe.

The Reich Spins the Welles Mission

Although Welles' arrival in Berlin was censored in Germany, the same German government was sending up trial balloons by way of planted press reports intended to be picked up in the foreign press. One widely distributed story, originating in Dublin, was filled with rampant speculation on what was going on behind the scenes diplomatically. The details of the story brazenly give it away as diplomatic intrigue on the part of the German government. The intent was to spin the Welles mission to their own advantage. Since Welles was not supposed to be accepting or making any proposals, the German government decided to take their proposals directly to the public in the west.

On March 1, 1940, reports began to surface that Germany had a new peace plan to present to the British and French governments. In connection with the Welles mission, Germany was proposing the creation of a new Polish state, self-administration for the Czechs, the return of former German colonies, and a general disarmament conference.

According to the story, the German diplomatic legation in Dublin was the source. They supposedly had been instructed to submit the peace plan to Lord Tavistock, who, in turn, would pass it on to Lord Halifax at the British Foreign Office. The terms of this proposal included the recreation of an independent Poland with access to the sea, the establishment of a free Czech state, a disarmament conference, the return of Germany's former colonies, and Germany's return to the League of Nations.

The story goes on to claim that Tavistock met with Halifax at the British Foreign Office. Halifax is said to have suggested that Germany prove its good intentions by evacuating Czech and Polish territory immediately. The *New York Times* version of this story claimed that a "Foreign Office spokesman" admitted that this was one among many similar peace proposals from German sources, but that this particular proposal was unique because it was the only one claiming any direct connection to the German government.[205] In a strange twist, the Reich envoy to Ireland denied being the source of any peace plan the very next day.[206]

Welles and Weizsäcker

Upon Welles' arrival, German State Secretary Weizsäcker warned him that Ribbentrop would do his best to stand in the way of any constructive approach to peace. Weizsäcker told Welles that he believed that the person most likely able to mollify Hitler's position was Mussolini. Welles was encouraged by Weizsäcker's insight because it corresponded with Roosevelt's and his own. Welles indicated Roosevelt's inclination to use Mussolini's influence to get Hitler to reconsider taking the war to the next level in a rather roundabout way and without mentioning any specifics. However, Weizsäcker was clever enough to fill in the details that had been carefully left out. The German State Secretary appreciated the possibility that the US government was seeking to use Mussolini to talk some sense into Hitler. He knew that Hitler was intending to launch a massive western offensive in the near future, and he could think of no better way of getting Hitler to reconsider this move other than Mussolini's direct and persistent influence.[207]

Before Welles' conversation with Weizsäcker ended, he was once more advised to somehow bypass Ribbentrop. Of course, there was *no way* that Welles could avoid the scheduled meeting with the German foreign minister, irrespective of his instinct that the meeting would yield next to nothing productive.

Welles and Ribbentrop

As expected, Welles' meeting with Ribbentrop was a dead end. Apparently, Ribbentrop was rather "undiplomatic" in his treatment of Welles.[208]

Welles did his best to relay the purpose of his mission to the rather aloof foreign minister, despite the fact that Welles found Ribbentrop's personal demeanor personally repugnant.

He informed Ribbentrop that it was Roosevelt's wish to "ascertain whether there existed a possibility of the establishment of a sound and permanent peace in Europe." The US Undersecretary of State qualified this statement by underscoring the fact that the US government was not "interested in any precarious or temporary peace."[209]

After a lengthy polemic by Ribbentrop on recent history, in which he placed the blame squarely on the British for the demise of Poland, the German foreign minister deployed the ace up his sleeve. Ribbentrop claimed that he had "incontrovertible proof" that the British purposefully stood in the way of a peaceful settlement between German and Poland over the question of rejoining the majority-German areas of Poland to the Reich.

After a momentary pause, the embittered German statesman stared in an accusing fashion at Welles in a way that implied that the US had been involved and could not be trusted. Although Welles seems to have been taken by surprise, he later figured out what Ribbentrop had been talking about. He was referring to the communications that took place in which Roosevelt, through the US ambassadors to Poland and France, had pressured the Polish government *not* to negotiate with Germany on the issue.[210]

The meeting seems to have come to an end when Welles had heard enough of Ribbentrop's haranguing on the parallels between the US Monroe Doctrine and Germany's new position in eastern Europe. Ribbentrop essentially accused the US government of hypocrisy, citing that Germany had never interfered in the US sphere of influence.[211]

Welles Meets the German Führer

On March 2, Welles, accompanied by the American chargé d'affaires in Berlin, Alexander Kirk, visited Hitler at the New Chancellery on the Wilhemstrasse. After detailing the purpose of his mission to Hitler, Welles breached the subject of the possibility of a peaceful solution. "I spoke only of a just peace," Welles reported later. Of a peace that would assure "stability and security" for the future.[212]

As the conversation developed the Nazi-German version of a "just" peace came to the fore; namely, that Versailles had created artificial states, and that it was intolerable for the Allies to sustain these states by military guarantees and economic treaties.

Hitler admitted that his position had become intransigent due to the fact that his calls for peace had been rejected. He told Welles that he felt that the source of Allied intransigence was their inability to recognize that there was no real distinction between National Socialism and the German people. Hitler tried to convince Welles that this factor was the mindset ultimately standing in the way of peace. He just could not get over that the British and French had decided to treat his government as illegitimate. The German chancellor could not understand what purpose would exist for him to draw a distinction between the British people and their government. Hitler held the Allies' refusal to deal with his regime as the leading factor standing in the way of peace.

By this equation, Hitler attempted to convince Welles that the Allies obviously wanted the destruction of *Germany*, saying that he "could see no hope for the establishment of any lasting peace until the will of England and France to destroy Germany is itself destroyed."[213]

Hitler seems to have taken pains to emphasize his desire "to reach an amicable and lasting understanding with England." Welles got an earful of the Führer's take on recent history, and the right of the German Reich for a free hand in central and eastern Europe, based on its "historical position of a thousand years." The fundamental gist of this lecture was that "Germany could not tolerate the existence of a state such as Czechoslovakia which constituted an enclave created by Versailles solely for strategic reasons, and which formed an ever-present menace to the security of the German people; nor could Germany tolerate the separation from Greater Germany of German provinces by corridors, under alien control." Hitler protested that Nazi Germany did not wish to rule over non-German people, and that as long as those notions were not a threat to Germany their independence was secure.[214]

A Necessary Aside: What Nazism Implied for the Future

What Hitler meant by this was that the Poles, Czechs, Hungarians, Slovaks, Lithuanians, etc. would be able to retain their political independence as long as these nations conformed to Hitler's strict ethnographic concepts. Economic arrangements were important, but secondary to Hitler. It goes without saying that Hitler's vision of the future in Europe entailed a tightly segregated set of nations, whose only right to exist was based on the premise that nation equaled race and ethnicity. Any other definition of "nation state," by logical extension, was ultimately unacceptable to Hitler.

However, there was a notable exception in Hitler's world view. What of the "Pan" question—Pan-Germanism, Pan-Slavism, etc? Hitler and other leading Nazis already envisioned a day when the term "German" was less important than "Aryan" or "Germanic." The logical extension of this expansion implied the threat of an ever-widening scope of *Nazi* influence. In other words, if Germany sought to redraw the map of Europe based on racist identity theory, was there ever an end in sight to this revisionism? After all, it was well known that the Nazis regarded the Norwegians, Swedes, Finns, Dutch, Swiss, British, French, etc. as their "Germanic brothers."

When in retrospect US Secretary of State Cordell Hull said, "Peace at [that] time would be equivalent to German victory—even if the Germans made some major concessions," he was on to something of major significance. Making peace with Germany at that time would have been tantamount to a *Nazi* victory—a victory of Hitler's vision. Even if Hitler had made far-reaching concessions, Nazism and all it implied would retain its stranglehold on the future of Europe—and perhaps the world.[215]

Welles' talk with Hitler made it obvious that the Nazi warlord completely understood the major premise of Allied intransigence. He was right in believing that Allied intransigence was founded on a rebellion against the extension of the most fundamental principles of "Hitlerism." Hitlerism to the Allies was nothing more than Nazi domestic policy being applied to German foreign policy.[216]

It was because of this most basic ideological difference, inextricably bound to the requirement for "justice" based on "security," verses "justice" based on the resolution of the "nationalities question," that the members of the Roosevelt administration, in the end, felt that "nothing he [Welles] learned gave us any basis for action" or "real hope for peace."[217]

Hitler's statement to Welles, emphasizing "his desire to reach an understanding with England" was appraised by FDR as being an attempt by Hitler to undermine the Allied will to war.[218] The President had reacted similarly to Hitler's peace proposals back in October of 1939. Now Roosevelt was himself participating in an attempt to make Hitler feel insecure about the prospects of taking the military initiative against the Allies by way of the Welles mission. It was Roosevelt who desired to drive a wedge between the Axis partners and thereby undermine *Germany's* will to war. Roosevelt believed he was simply out-Hitlering Hitler. Even though Welles was in the midst of a mission to ostensibly pursue any leads that might lead to a real peace, the American President was already convinced that a real shooting war was inevitable. FDR was firmly in the Allied camp. He thought that a peace with a victorious Hitler would be a "patched-up" peace, simply because Hitler would retain his monopoly on the future.[219]

Welles Meets with Göring

Welles went on to meet with Herman Göring at his private residence, Karinhall, on Sunday, March 3, 1940. Göring seems to have gone out of his way to emphasize to Welles his puzzlement over France's unexpected support for Poland's resistance on the question of uniting the German populations of western Poland to the Reich. The German Reichsminister told Welles that in Munich, during the resolution of the Sudetenland crisis, "Monsieur Bonnet [the French foreign minister] had expressly renounced any political interest in eastern Europe. Göring insisted that Bonnet had "specifically agreed not to influence Poland against the conclusion of an agreement with Germany whereby Danzig would return to Germany, and Germany would receive an extraterritorial corridor from East Prussia to Greater Germany."[220] Göring was obviously trying to make the case to Welles that German foreign policy had been consistent in its desire to incorporate German minorities living under the control of surrounding foreign nations, whereas the British and French had been inconsistent and had sent mixed signals. The clear implication is that Göring felt that the Allied guarantee of military assistance to Poland had been reckless and irresponsible. He held this guarantee responsible for the general war, because it had emboldened the Polish government and stiffened its resistance to a negotiated settlement of the German minorities problem.

What Göring's argument did not take into account was the question of *why* British and French policy had changed—or, as he claimed, was "inconsistent." The answer from the Allied point of view was obvious. When Germany's revisionist foreign policy became inconsistent itself, things changed. In the case of the Sudetenland, the Nazi government appeared to have used the German minorities question as leverage to take in other territories *not* dominated by German populations. Germany had gone beyond the spirit as well as the letter of the Munich Agreement, and had swallowed up the Czech homeland.

Welles patiently let this glaring inconsistency on Göring's part slide.

Göring followed up his original statements by presenting Welles with a list of elements that he believed represented a starting point for general negotiations to end the war. This list included:

1. Austria, the Sudetenland, and all of the portions of the former Polish state inhabited by Germans must be retained by the Reich.

2. Germany would remain in occupation of Bohemia-Moravia and Poland until a formal peace was made with the western Allies.

3. If peace came, the Czechs would be granted political independence on a demilitarized basis.

4. Poland would be granted an independent existence. The Polish state that could be resurrected must be drawn up on strictly ethnographic lines, but would be given access to the sea.

5. Germany, for economic reasons, should have her former colonies restored. The colonies that Göring said had been "pilfered" from Germany by the infamous Versailles Treaty.

6. British and French recognition of Germany's position of "economic preeminence" in eastern Europe.[221]

On the heels of Göring's outline, Welles handed the Reichsmarschal a memorandum from the Roosevelt administration, concerning possible future international trade policies. Göring stated that he "was entirely in accord with every word" in the document, and that the German government would "whole-heartedly cooperate" in the effort to restore the free flow of international trade as a part of the general peace negotiations.[222]

At this juncture, Göring seems to have changed the subject. He wanted to talk about the Allies' war objectives. Göring told Welles that he was "completely convinced" that the Allies were out "to destroy the German regime," to "subjugate the German people," and to "split Germany into small units under military control." Once again, Welles found the same old line. Göring said that the Allies' vision of a "lasting peace" was meant to be achieved on the basis of Germany's return to its fragmented nineteenth-century status.[223] Göring was doubtful that any solution, short of eradicating the Allies' desire to destroy Germany, would stand any chance of success.

Welles did go on to meet with Rudolf Hess, the head of the Nazi Party, and the man who had been Hitler's second-in-command. The US Undersecretary of State's memoir and his notes in the FDR Presidential Library on this meeting do not indicate that anything of real significance took place at the meeting.

On to France and Premier Daladier

On March 7, 1940, Welles arrived in Paris, chatted briefly with President LeBrun, and then was taken by the French Secret Service to see the Prime

Minister. Welles' dialogue with Daladier provides an illustration of the Allied notion of justice based on security. As in President Roosevelt's case, this security notion found its origin in the German-Czechoslovakian crisis.[224]

Welles did not waste much time getting down to the most important question. He asked the French premier for his views concerning "the possibilities for the negotiation now of a just and lasting peace." Daladier was assured by Welles that any "discussion of French peace objectives" would be kept "entirely confidential." What the French premier would be willing to convey to Welles was for the US President's and US Secretary of State Hull's ears alone.[225]

Daladier stressed that independence must be restored for the Poles and Czechs. He qualified this initial peace objective by saying that it was completely reasonable to allow the Germans of Central Europe to live under German rule. He cited Danzig as an example, admitting that it was obviously a German city—as were the Sudeten Germans and the Germans of western Poland [the Polish Corridor].[226] To be consistent, Daladier related that the French government would accept the continued union of Germany and Austria, provided an "impartial plebiscite" be conducted in Austria.[227]

Most remarkable of all is what is found in one part of Welles' written summary of his meeting with Daladier. According to Welles,

> The Prime Minister made it very clear to me that he did not believe, whatever he might say in public, he would not refuse to deal with the present German regime....[228]

However, Daladier had to point out his deep-seated distrust of Hitler, due to the inconsistency of German foreign policy. Daladier recalled how Hitler had assured him "that the German people would never consent to defile the purity of the German race by incorporating Bohemia and Moravia [the Czechs] in Greater Germany at the time of the Munich Conference."[229] Hitler's actions thereafter contradicted his stated philosophy and his word. This experience allowed Daladier to relate the plight of Czechoslovakia and Poland to the future issue of French security. For example, the last two diplomatic crises were over the question of the repatriation of majority-German territories in Czechoslovakia and Poland. What about the Alsace and Lorraine question in France then? Would not Hitler's Nazi philosophy lead him to make demands of France next?

Daladier's question is more than vaguely reminiscent of British Prime Minister Chamberlain's words in the House of Commons back in April of 1939, when he was trying to explain how the Munich Agreement had gone wrong:

Assurances…had been given me…that they [the German government] had no wish to dominate other races, and that all they wanted was to assimilate Germans living in territories adjacent to their country…. These assurances have been thrown to the winds.[230]

With a consistency that is striking, as Welles went on to talk with other top French leaders, such as Bonnet, Reynaud, and Blum, the central point in each of these men's arguments hit upon the same question of security within the context of *Hitler's inconsistency.*[231] Welles' conversations with these men seemed to inevitably shift in the direction of outlining the differences between French and German interpretations of a "just" solution to the war. For this reason, the issue of peace is secondary. No just peace without security could be had as far as the leading figures of the French government were concerned. Welles' version of his conversation with Leon Blum is typical:

In his crowded and charming study we talked for a long time of the events of the two years since I had last seen him, and of the tragically swift collapse of the cardboard structure of international security.[232]

Roosevelt Scolds the French

Welles' final contact with the French government during his mission involved the delivering of a personal letter from FDR to France's Minister of Finance, Paul Reynaud. Welles personally handed Reynaud Roosevelt's letter. In this letter, the American President expressed his conviction that economics was the main culprit in the outbreak of hostilities in Europe. Cited by Roosevelt was the tendency toward "bilateralism" and "discriminatory arrangements" among European nations. The President, was, in effect, scolding the French government for isolating Germany and especially Italy economically. The letter implied that unwise economic policy had not only isolated Germany, but that it had forced Italy into a necessary relationship with Germany. Furthermore, the President held these unfair economic practices responsible for generating the desire in Germany and Italy to achieve autarky. Roosevelt was firm in his faith that economic autarky leads directly to political autocracy. He was equally under the conviction that the future of a peaceful Europe would have to be based on the concept of free and open trade, unfettered access and competition for raw materials. In short, *economic interdependency* in Europe would lead to a more permanent peace, because it would be in the interest of all nations to keep the goods rolling in and out. FDR even went so far as to intimate that economic bilateralism was the root cause of the creation of the senseless alliance system that had triggered a war of territorial revision. FDR really believed that wars of territorial revision could be made a thing of the past if all nations had equal, free, and unfettered access to raw materials, goods and services.[233]

On to London and Prime Minister Chamberlain

On the morning of March 11, Welles took a cross-channel flight to London, escorted by French combat planes. After visiting the king and queen at Buckingham Palace, and chatting with Lord Halifax, Welles went to 10 Downing Street with US Ambassador Joseph Kennedy to meet with the Prime Minister.

Neville Chamberlain was a statesman who oozed with the emotions of someone who felt betrayed. Hitler had betrayed his good offices once, and he would not get away with it again. Chamberlain was solid on one point—peace would not be possible until Germany was "forced to restore complete independence to the Polish people," and to "reconstitute a free and independent Czechia." Moreover, Chamberlain did not believe that Hitler wanted peace—not a *real* peace. He was weary of the constant menace posed by Nazi to the other smaller, surrounding, nations in Europe. What Hitler wanted was "a Europe dominated by German Hitlerism."

As the Prime Minister spoke, his confidence in the righteousness of the cause against Hitlerism grew by leaps and bounds. In reading Welles' account of the meeting, one can practically feel Chamberlain's convictions, when he remarked that the concepts of liberty and democracy were "threatened with extinction" by "Hitlerism."[234]

Mr. Chamberlain related to Welles his unshakable conviction, "with red hot anger," that Hitler "did not desire a peaceful Europe founded upon justice, reason, and security."[235] In this belief, Chamberlain was right on target. It was indeed true that Hitler did not seek peace based upon Chamberlain's version of justice and security. That does not mean, however, that Hitler had not wanted to end the war in the west. Hitler wanted what Chamberlain referred to as a "patched-up peace." Once Hitler had gained his diplomatic objective of getting Britain and France to swear off eastern Europe, there can be no doubt that the German sword would have been turned on the vast expanses of the USSR—as had always been the objective.

Dinner Guests

Later that evening, Welles dined with Lord Halifax. After dinner, Halifax conducted what Welles calls in his memoirs a "seminar" in the drawing room. The American Undersecretary of State found himself in front of a small audience of leading British statesmen. One at a time, these special guests expressed various views. These opinions regarding a negotiated peace with

Germany were quite diverse. Welles recalls Lord Stanley's suggestion that the German people had to be "taught a lesson." They must be dealt a crushing military defeat on their own soil—otherwise their basic character would never change. There were, of course people who were probably ready to negotiate a peace under the present condition represented at the "seminar" as well. What becomes obvious, when reading Welles' notes of the evening, is that British official opinion was deeply divided.[236]

Churchill at the Admiralty

The next afternoon, Welles met with Winston Churchill at the Admiralty. Not surprisingly, Churchill was perhaps the most intransigent figure he had encountered so far. The First Lord of the Admiralty saw things in black and white. To him, the Germans were the same people whose basic nature was unchanged. They were the same people who he had faced during the First World War. All the Germans wanted was "world supremacy and military conquest." What Germany wanted constituted an ever present and continuing threat to the security of the British Empire, the United States, and the rest of the world. They must be stopped by force. All they understand is the language of force. Therefore, Churchill outlined his roadmap to peace to Welles in the following terms:

1. The complete defeat of Germany.
2. The destruction of National Socialism.
3. The reconstitution of Austria, Poland and Czechoslovakia.
4. The end of "German hegemony" in Central Europe.

What about the USSR? Did Churchill have any choice words for Welles about Germany's accomplice in the dismemberment of the Poland that Churchill wanted re-created? Amazingly, Churchill seems to have made only one statement on the Soviets. Welles' notes on the meeting offer this solitary comment:

Russia, to him [Churchill], offered no real menace and no real problem.[237]

An Assortment of Opinions

Lest one be left under the mistaken impression that there were not influential politicians who found themselves in fundamental discord with Chamberlain and Churchill, the case of James Maxton should be considered.

Maxton was a wily "dissident member" of the Labour Party who desired, and was granted, an audience with Welles. Maxton told Welles that he was in favor of ending the war immediately. He described the pending threat of another World War as a "criminal blunder." Peace negotiations should begin at once![238]

Although it might be tempting to portray Maxton's views as being well out of the mainstream, former Prime Minister David Lloyd George took a remarkably similar line with Welles, saying that the present war was:

> …the most unnecessary war, the most insanely stupid war, that had ever been forced upon England. He [Lloyd George] said that Great Britain had blundered into this war because of the egregious mistakes in the policy of her recent governments. He stated that there was no reason, from the standpoint of either Great Britain or France, why Germany should not obtain and enjoy a special economic position in Central Europe, and, at least in part of Southeastern Europe.
>
> All in all, it was his opinion that no policy could have been more criminally stupid than that pursued by the present Allies toward Germany in recent years.[239]

Welles met with other notables in London, including Sir Archibald Sinclair, the leader of the Liberal Party in the House of Commons, and the Labor Party leader, Major Clement Attlee. For Attlee, the war was necessary on moral grounds. Peace could be made with "any government of Germany," provided solid guarantees of real security and independence for the nations of Europe could be made. For Sinclair, there could be "no compromise with Hitler." "Hitlerism" had to be extinguished "root and branch." Sinclair admitted to Welles that the only way to accomplish this objective was through total Allied victory.[240]

An Unscheduled Meeting with Reynaud

Two days later Welles was back in France again. He was stopping there on his way back to Rome. Someone was curious about what Welles got out of his visit to London.

Paul Reynaud was so curious that he made an unscheduled visit to Welles. The French Secretary of the Treasury cornered Welles at his Parisian hotel shortly before leaving to catch the train for Rome.

Reynaud was direct and got down to business. He wanted to know what Welles thought about the attitudes he had encountered in London regarding the chances for peace.

Before Welles had the opportunity to go into any detail, Reynaud interrupted, saying that Churchill had "just paid him a midnight visit two nights before." That would have been the same night after Welles' conference with Churchill. Reynaud portrayed Churchill's position as "utterly intransigent," and inflexible. It seems to have frightened Reynaud that Churchill could see nothing less than a "war to the finish." Welles characterizes Reynaud's final words to him before they parted:

> The minister twice repeated his conviction that the possibility of negotiation on the basis of security and disarmament should not be discarded.[241]

What was required above all else, said Reynaud, would be "daring statesmanship."

Back to Rome

Before Welles landed in Paris on the first leg of his return to Rome, the Finns had capitulated to the Soviets. An armistice was requested by the Finnish government and accepted by Stalin on March 13. The Finnish problem had been solved and the British Foreign Office was "secretly relieved," because the British Expeditionary Force destined for Scandinavia had been "ready to sail."[242]

Upon Welles' return to Rome on March 16, according to his own notes of the meeting, he went out of his way to tell the Italian foreign minister, Ciano, that Mussolini had been totally wrong in believing that the same mood of intransigence prevailed in London and Paris as in Berlin. What is unusual about Welles' initial comments to Ciano is simple. It is not backed up by *his experiences*. Welles' notes do not reveal any greater intransigence on one side than the other. So, why did Welles say this to Ciano?

A slightly different version of Welles' impression of Allied intransigence is given by Ciano. The Ciano diary of March 16, 1940, states that Welles intimated that if the Allies "had guarantees of security, they would give in, and accept the fait accompli [of the Polish war]." This version more accurately squares with the situation on two levels:

1. The words used in Ciano's account find resonance in Welles' notes from his meetings with Daladier, Reynaud, and Lloyd George.

2. The Allies had accepted *Soviet* de facto absorption of Polish territory and were working to *avoid war* with the USSR once they switched the war with Germany to Scandinavia.[243]

Ribbentrop's Intervention

While Welles had been in London, the German foreign minister, Ribbentrop,[244] had been canvassing Mussolini with all possible energy. Ciano at once told Welles of this fact and admitted that due to certain circumstances and Ribbentrop's influence, "Mussolini was definitely pro-German" at the moment.[245] Ribbentrop had actually delivered Hitler's long-awaited response to the Mussolini letter of January 4, 1940. Mussolini's letter had urged Hitler to come to terms with the Allies. Now, according to Paul Schmidt, the interpreter present at the Ribbentrop-Mussolini conference, "Mussolini was definitely pro-war."[246]

Actually, Ribbentrop's mission to Rome is only part of the reason for Mussolini's change of attitude. Britain had decided to again restrict the flow of Italian coal, which forced the Italian government to cut a deal with Germany to have the supplies shipped overland through Germany.[247] Ribbentrop had also been tasked with making Mussolini understand what the Allies were up to. Specifically, that the Allies were working behind the scenes to woo the Soviets and spread the war to Scandinavia as a sideshow intended to sap the strength of the German forces. That the Allies were working to drive a wedge between the Axis partners—probably with the covert assistance of Roosevelt's envoy—Welles.

Ribbentrop argued that the British government's mission to Moscow, headed by Sir Stafford Cripps, was connected to Welles' return to Rome.[248] Ribbentrop presented the Duce with some peculiar "inside information" regarding what Welles had *really* been up to while he was visiting Paris and London. Ribbentrop had "proof" that Welles had been sharing the supposedly "confidential information" gathered in Rome and Berlin and had personally passed it on to his Allied confidants in Paris and Rome.

Mussolini could scarcely believe that he had been taken in by such a scheme. First, Mussolini reasoned, he would put Welles to the test. The Italian dictator questioned Welles during their meeting but had quickly shifted the conversation to "confide" something of grave importance. The crafty Duce told Welles that the German offensive against France was "at hand." After sharing this "confidential information" with Welles, Mussolini figured that if Roosevelt really desired peace instead of merely wishing to drive a wedge between Italy and Germany, then Welles would be willing to share information that he had learned from the Allies as well. Mussolini asked Welles if he would be willing to share any impressions that he had gained in his visits to Berlin, Paris, and London that could be used to avert the impending disaster. Mussolini also said that he would be willing to "answer any questions" if Welles would fill him in on some important details. But when Welles countered by saying that "the views expressed by the heads of governments…in the countries which I [have] visited must be regarded as strictly confidential," Mussolini felt that Welles had fallen into the most obvious trap. After all, if Welles could not share *anything* with him, what *was he doing* in Rome again, anyway?[249]

Welles' response severely undermined Mussolini's confidence in Welles' impartiality and the mission's intentions. It confirmed the seed planted by Ribbentrop—that Welles was actually representing the belligerent attitudes of a President who could not effect a desired foreign policy due to American domestic, political considerations, and the strictures of the neutrality legislation passed by the US Congress.

The final, damning confirmation of Welles' "scheming," in Mussolini's mind, came by way of a picture published in the French periodical *L'Illustration*. The title page of this publication sported a photo of Sumner Welles and Paul Reynaud, in front of a radically re-drawn map of Europe. This bit of intelligence had come to Mussolini's attention by way of a group of pro-Nazi members of the Italian Fascist Council. Roberto Farinacci of the Regime Fascista had been quick to point out to Mussolini, and then the foreign press, that this map was an Allied postwar plan for Europe. It represented the Allies' vision for a "just" and "lasting peace." This was like a slap in Welles' face. The clearly visible map that appeared in the background behind Welles and Reynaud showed a divided-up *Italy*—not just Germany![250]

Welles had indeed shared information gained in other capitals despite his protestations to the contrary to the Duce.[251] In fact, Ivan Maisky, the Soviet ambassador in London, learned from R.A. Butler, who had been informed by Welles, of the details of Welles' discussion with Hitler.[252]

German intelligence had hard evidence that Welles told the British Prime Minister that a German offensive should be expected in the near future.[253] Furthermore, Welles had asked the British if they had any inside information on Ribbentrop's recent meetings with Mussolini and the Pope.[254] Indeed, there seemed to be no information that Welles shared with Axis leadership, other than to report to Ciano that the Allies had been much less intransigent than the Duce had supposed. Unfortunately, for Welles, Welles lost all credibility with Mussolini. Ribbentrop had beaten him to the punch.

The End of a Mission

As a fitting end to the Welles mission, after the US Undersecretary of State had spoken to Mussolini for the last time, he related the "Chief Points" of his interview with the Duce by cross-Atlantic telephone to President Roosevelt. Welles called Roosevelt to ask for his authorization to officially seek Mussolini's assistance in an approach to Hitler. FDR responded in the negative. The US President did not want his actions to be misconstrued by the Allies. He feared that the Allies would interpret the use of Mussolini as a mediator for peace as an attempt to begin to negotiate a peace on Hitler's terms. Roosevelt wanted Welles to communicate to Mussolini the President's conviction that "the problem of security was the fundamental issue."[255]

Thereafter, Welles remained in Rome until after a meeting between Hitler and Mussolini at the Brenner Pass. He gleaned from the Italian foreign minister, Ciano, the details of what transpired. Welles departed for home with the certain knowledge that the possibility of "driving a wedge between the two madmen" was rapidly disappearing. He left Italy without any clear impression regarding Italy's future role in a conflict that seemed more inevitable than ever.

Later, during the darkest days of Germany's onslaught against the Allied forces in France, on the day that Italy finally became a belligerent, Roosevelt made a solemn yet eloquent statement of US foreign policy objectives. Nestled within FDR's speech to a University of Virginia crowd, were some remarkable reflections on the Welles mission.

The President recalled that Mussolini had first sent word that the Italian government desired to limit the war. Roosevelt placed this event as taking place "more that three months ago." This means that it took place before February 10, 1940, when Roosevelt made the official announcement of the Welles mission. The Duce's notion, Roosevelt continued, met with the sympathy of the US government, and the Italian head of state was notified forthwith. After a reflective pause, the President went on to describe, "On a subsequent occasion, not so long ago…I offered, in a message addressed to the Chief of the Italian government, to send to the governments of France and Great Britain" a proposal to "obtain readjustments" concerning Italy's "position." FDR then revealed that if Italy had remained neutral, he would have been willing to work on behalf of the Duce to procure a guarantee "that Italy's voice in any future peace conference would have the same authority as if Italy had actually taken part in the war as a belligerent."[256]

The statement by President Roosevelt, March 29, 1930:

> Under Secretary of State Welles has concluded the mission which he was sent to Europe and has reported to me and to the Secretary of State.
>
> As I said when the announcement of Mr. Welles' mission was made, Mr. Welles was sent to Europe in order to obtain information with regard to the existing conditions. He was neither authorized to make, nor has he made, any commitments involving the government of the United States, nor was he empowered, to offer, and he has not offered, any proposals in the name of this government. He has not

received, nor has he brought back to me, any peace proposals from any source.

The information which he has received from the heads of the governments which he has visited will be of the greatest value to this government in the general conduct of its foreign relations. As was announced at the time of his departure from the United States, the information communicated to him by the Italian, German, French, and British governments will be regarded as entirely confidential by this government. It relates to the views and policies of the Europe's government's mentioned."

"...Finally, even though there may be scant immediate prospect for the establishment of any just, stable, and lasting peace in Europe, the information made available to this government as a result of Mr. Welles' mission will undoubtedly be of the greatest value when the time comes for the establishment of such a peace.[257]

Some Analysis of the Welles Mission

In the final analysis, the Welles mission is most significant because it propelled the Allies to hold on to their assumptions of a just peace based on security. It cemented the Axis notion of a just peace based on the solving of the national minorities question. It introduced the Roosevelt administration to a more-full psychology of Allied intransigence. Whether or not it can be proved that Welles' peace mission was really intended to drive a wedge between the Axis partners is ultimately irrelevant, because there is no doubt that the mission confirmed Roosevelt's extant notions—which paralleled the Allied vision of the future of Europe. If FDR could use his influence to keep Italy from entering the war, perhaps Germany would refrain from launching an offensive. Perhaps, the Allies could more easily achieve a military victory. Perhaps, no big offensive would be launched by either side because of the diversionary campaigns that Roosevelt knew were about to be initiated by the Allies. Perhaps if Welles had succeeded in "driving a wedge between the two madmen," Chamberlain's Peace Front strategy might have had enough time to *really* work. In any case, the best way to achieve Roosevelt's vision of the establishment of a lasting peace was to do his best to decrease Germany's chances of victory. Yes, Roosevelt was partial. To the President, the very concept of "peace" was partial. Only one compatible vision of the future existed to Roosevelt. The choice presented to the US President was simple. He could work as a silent partner of the western Allies, while remaining neutral—so the United States could play the role of mediator for the new and improved version of the Versailles Treaty. Alternatively, he could disengage diplomatically from the situation—and thereby forfeit any real leverage for achieving the sort of peace that was best designed to avoid the specter of world war from rising again.

No more appropriate words were written about the Welles mission than the following quote by Sumner Welles himself at the end of his trip. They demonstrate that his mission was as a microcosm of the general situation in Europe.

Of all the many statements made to me in the conversations I had, the statement which I have most often recalled is the phrase used by Paul Reynaud in my final talk with him, when he said, 'If the catastrophe is to be averted, daring statesmanship is required.' That, I believe, is unquestionably true. If the present situation continues to drift, no matter whether a war of devastation breaks out in the immediate future or not, I doubt whether the present generation will again see a world in which there exists any real security, national, physical, or economic.

What is imperatively required is statesmanship of the highest character, marked by vision, courage and daring.

I saw no signs of statesmanship of that kind in any of the countries I visited, nor do I know of any of that character in any other European country.[258]

CHAPTER THREE

Peace Prospects
After the Fall of France

We let ourselves be carried along on the tide of events; we made neither peace nor war.
> —French Foreign Minister Georges Bonnet

Hitler had followed up his defeat of France with a new peace offer to Britain, now in military isolation. Churchill's rejection of this offer was to be explained not least by statements communicated to London by the American President. This and other actions by Roosevelt compelled Hitler to conclude that the US's government intended to enter the war at a suitable time.
> —German Foreign Minister Joachim von Ribbentrop

I should also describe how Stalin reacted when Hitler moved against France. The French and British troops were defeated....I remember Stalin. He was extremely nervous...He cursed the French. He cursed the English. How could they allow Hitler to defeat them, to crush them?
> —Khrushchev, quoting Stalin.[259]

The Blitz on France

When the German offensive finally came on May 10, 1940, it was decisive. The combined arms military strategy, commonly known as "Blitzkrieg," swept the forces of Britain, France, and the Benelux countries from the field of battle in merely six weeks' time!

German military strategy and execution was nearly flawless when one considers that they were actually outnumbered and outgunned in all categories. The German blitz had also been the death-knell of Chamberlain's Peace Front strategy. As the full strength of Germany's offensive began to take form, it became obvious that this policy had been far from effective or timely. Along with the shock of German Panzers and screaming Stukas came the toppling of the French political structure. On the British side, the bulk of its expeditionary force escaped across the English Channel to safety after a desperate retreat. The French forces were not so fortunate. The decision was made to ask the Germans for an armistice.

With the capitulation of the Allied forces in France and the signing of the Franco-German armistice on June 22, 1940, it is tempting to conclude that both sides might seriously consider sheathing their war daggers.

Could peace have been achieved between Great Britain and the Third Reich after France's capitulation? If so, who thought it possible? Who desired peace at this juncture? What proposals to end the war existed? Were any terms ever offered?

To answer these questions one must start by exploring the backup plans formulated by the British government in the event of a military catastrophe. It would seem sensible that the famously thorough British War Cabinet considered a contingency plan in case France broke its promise not to make any separate armistice or peace.[260]

A Backup Plan

Incredibly, the British did create a backup plan, relatively late in the French campaign. Lord Hankey, along with the British State Secretary for Foreign Affairs, drew up the plan. This document, entitled "Action by His Majesty's Government in the Event of a French Military Collapse," was presented to the British War Cabinet on May 27, 1940. The Hankey Report considered two scenarios. Consideration was given to whether or not France might continue the war from the British Isles, "or some other French Colony." The Hankey Report then went on to handle the question of what to do in the event that "the present French government or its successor might make peace with Germany."[261] For both eventualities the plan recommended that every possible effort should be made to make sure that all the important equipment, raw materials, wealth, and, if possible, political leadership did not fall into German hands. The British were especially fearful that the French navy would be used by the Germans in the prosecution of an invasion of Great Britain. Or, perhaps, a captive French navy could be used by the Germans to intimidate the British into negotiating an armistice.

In terms of this "most important item," the Hankey Report considered, in the case that the first scenario became a reality, there would be no problem in securing the French fleet. In the latter case, the assumption was that

Hitler's armistice terms would be harsh—including the handing over of the French fleet. In this case "the First Sea Lord [thought] it would be better if the French fleet were sunk before the emergency arises...." and that "at the appropriate time...he will get in touch with Admiral Darlan with a view to inducing him to sink the French fleet."[262]

The overriding assumption of the Hankey plan was that Hitler would desire to humiliate the French by imposing terms on her, roughly analogous to those imposed on Germany at the close of World War I—including a parallel to the handing over of the German fleet in 1918–1919. Of additional significance was the plan's assumption that the war with Germany would continue. The plan assumed that Hitler would push for an all-out invasion of the British Isles.

Could it be that not a single member of the British higher echelon considered that Hitler might want to end the war and come to an agreement? Were there members of the British government who wanted an armistice? Or was the notion of coming to *any* peaceful settlement with Hitlerite Germany simply *out of the question*?

A Necessary Aside on Revisionism

Before attempting to answer any of the questions raised above, a necessary aside is required to address any history that might be construed as being "revisionist." Unfortunately, to many, just asking the questions raised in the last paragraph is tantamount to some form of perfidy. The standard history of the period depicts an unwavering British government, headed by the indomitable Winston Churchill, who never allowed even the mention of the words "armistice" or "peace" in connection with "Hitler." This interpretation of events has served its purpose for over half a century—to steel the will of the eventual victors who would need it to win the peace in 1945, and then to sustain the western Allies during the long years of the cold war. Documentary evidence to the contrary rarely saw the light of day. The western Allies had a vested interest in releasing the documents that made it appear that Churchill and the British government never considered a parley with Hitler. The myth of a completely resolute British government, determined to fight on against all odds, provided a necessary psychological segway for the US's entry into the war on the side of the Allies. It is such a compelling faith that people are offended by any other interpretation of events. The fact is that this myth corresponds to the emotive forces of the day—the natural tendency to root for the little guy against the bully. Did most people, at the time, believe that Britain was faced with imminent invasion and perhaps destruction? The answer is, without question, "yes." Did most people, at the time, believe that Britain was "standing alone" against the greatest military machine ever constructed? Again, the answer is "yes." For these two reasons alone, many people are offended by the "revisionist" suggestion that Britain's stiff upper lip was not so stiff. This reaction is quite understandable. However, the myth was based on partial evidence, and, as any archaeologist who has discovered new evidence would point out, prior interpretations must be revised in light of new evidence. History must be pursued in the same fashion—when new evidence is found, new and fuller interpretations become a historian's responsibility. To do otherwise would be necessarily ignorant. On the other hand, "revisionist" can also imply that the writer is revising history to fit a particular political view or social construct—something that an objective historian should work tirelessly to avoid in order to be balanced in the pursuit of forming the most accurate picture of events. In this case, when it comes to the history of the Second World War, the prejudices of the political view of the victors is most often triumphant in the writing of history. Every once in a while some rogue historian might write from the perspective of the losers, of this there is no doubt.

On this last point, historians who try to remain aloof of political prejudice run the risk of being labeled as someone who supports the loser—a Nazi, a Fascist. By avoiding language that notifies the reader of the writers' political views, the historian inevitably makes enemies of every political ideology extant on the side of the victors. For instance, the unspoken attitude is quite visceral—if the historian is not obviously *for* me and my politics, then he must be *against* me and my politics. Of course, that is patent nonsense.

On yet another level another common argument exists against any revision of history. History as an art requires a certain passion and flair of expression to capture the reader's attention. Having a definite side to be on is the easy way out in respect to the Second World War. Being politically objective in writing about the most horrendous war in the history of mankind seems to take the luster right out of it all. However, as far as the author of this work is concerned, a politically detached history of the period can be achieved without losing the politically motivated "axe to grind" style of many historians. Namely, there is, or certainly ought to be, *passion* found in exploring the ways this odious war could have been stopped—short of the senseless annihilation of tens of millions of combatants and non-combatants alike!

Divided or Just Shell-Shocked?

There were members of the British government who knew that Hitler wanted to come to terms, and, in fact, had the inclination to initiate and/or open up channels for peace feelers.[263] Even Churchill thought that Britain might have to make peace with Germany if there was indisputable evidence that Germany was about to launch a decisive cross channel invasion, compounded by the absence of US or Soviet military assistance.

The British Prime Minister did not reject the notion of coming to terms with Hitler out of hand. Churchill told the members of his War Cabinet that as long as "matters vital to the independence" of the British Empire were untouched, he would be "thankful to get out of our present difficulties on such terms, provided that we retained the essential elements of our vital strength, even at the cost of some cession of territory."

The British War Cabinet did not agree on some fundamental issues. The largest division existed over what would be the "general policy in the event of things going really bad in France." French Premier Paul Reynaud had flown to London and met with the Churchill cabinet on May 26 and 27, 1940. In a series of sullen meetings, Reynaud painted a bleak picture of the military situation in France and made every effort to convince the Churchill government to use its influence to keep Italy out of the fray. But there was more. Halifax, Chamberlain, and Reynaud all agreed that perhaps Mussolini would be willing to serve as a mediator in a peace conference, since he had stayed out of the war even after Germany had launched its offensive. Indeed Halifax had related to the Italian ambassador to Britain, Bastionini, on May 25, that the British government was ready to entertain certain peace proposals. On the other hand, Churchill expressed the conviction that an approach to Mussolini would be useless. Useless on the grounds that Hitler's terms would likely entail the subjugation of the British Empire. He expected Hitler to be ruthless, so rabid in his demands, that Mussolini would just be a mute witness to any negotiations. What would be the point to retaining Mussolini's services, argued Churchill, the Italian dictator might even figure out a way to wrest from the Allies concessions for the benefit of Italy—even though Italy had not, to this point, fired a shot.

Churchill clashed with Halifax and others at the conference, holding the notion of a negotiated end to hostilities barely at arm's length. The military situation in France was nearly untenable as they spoke. Nevertheless, Churchill emphasized that the single most important test of the next few months would be the British government's ability to show the world that she remained intransigent and unbeaten. The defiant Prime Minister postulated that if Britain resisted "being dragged down the slippery slope with France," after a period of two or three months, confidence in Britain's ability to continue the struggle would return at home and abroad.[264]

Churchill felt he could avoid making peace by convincing his potential Allies that the British Empire could still make war. The British Prime Minister was not simply content to wait upon future developments though.

He was out to actively avoid the factors that would lead Britain down the "slippery slope."

So what did Churchill propose to do specifically? The answer can be found in the partial continuation of a policy that to the outside world seemed thoroughly discredited—Chamberlain's Peace Front policy. The Allies were near defeat in France—but not beaten. They had to hold out a bit longer in order to give the British government some breathing room in order to avoid the immense pressure for peace negotiations that were sure to come when France finally would go under.

Churchill worked furiously to resurrect the Roosevelt corollary to the Peace Front strategy. Similar assistance from the US government was desperately needed—the sort of assistance which had been attempted by Roosevelt by way of the Welles mission. Italy's good offices were not desired by Churchill to bring about peace negotiations. Rather, Churchill hoped to keep Italy from participating in the coming fall of France. Keeping Italy out of the war was essential.

Keep Him in the Game

On May 25, 1940, Churchill and Reynaud made a joint effort to encourage FDR to "make a further demarche toward Mussolini"—a suggestion which, of course, Roosevelt followed up on the very next day. The American President cabled a letter to the Duce, warning him to remain neutral. At the same time, the British government continued a policy designed to separate the Axis partners, by way of dangling concessions in Mussolini's face.[265] For a concerted effort, Roosevelt's services were desperately needed.

Churchill convinced the British War Cabinet that Roosevelt had to be given an active role in the process of courting Italy. The idea was bold and perhaps transparent, as far as Mussolini was concerned, but it *had* to be tried. Keeping Roosevelt in the game meant staving off any inclination that the US President might have to offer his own good offices to facilitate peace negotiations. The Americans had to be convinced that, even though France appeared to be a lost cause, armistice was *premature* as far as the British government was concerned.

Churchill had to stave off internal efforts to rope the American President into acting as a peace broker. For instance, an undated memorandum of the Australian High Commissioner, with a cover letter written by Desmond Morton, penned on May 30, suggested that Roosevelt be requested to call for an international conference "to formulate a peace settlement." When this document came to the British Prime Minister's attention, an obviously perturbed Churchill did not even take the time to formulate an officially typed response. Instead, with his own pen, he wrote the word "Rot" directly on the memo and scratched out the offending paragraph—placing the word "No" at the top.[266]

From the first signs of the German onslaught on France, the approach to the "American problem" was set in Churchill's mind. The British ambassador in Washington, Lothian, had been sending weekly political summaries of American attitudes regarding the possibility of US military intervention on the side of the Allies. Lord Lothian had been sending suggestions to the British War Cabinet and Foreign Office regarding what official line they should take. At the outbreak of the full-blown war on the western front, Lothian advised, "there is however no movement for intervention now, nor will there be until America's vital interests become affected."[267] The policy of the British government was to convince the American people that their vital interests would be in jeopardy if intervention were not forthcoming. Hopefully this could be achieved before the battle of France was lost. Even if American intervention were not timely, the efforts would not cease. On the contrary, it would have to be turned up a notch.

After the battle of France had been lost, British tactics had to be somewhat modified. The new goal was to convince Roosevelt and the American people that the British Empire was firmly committed to fighting to the bitter end. The Americans had to be convinced that Britain faced *imminent danger* and would likely go under. Perhaps the implications of a British defeat would frighten FDR enough to get him to commit the US to direct military intervention.

Churchill's plan to affect American interests had far-reaching implications, including the provocation of the Japanese. For example, the British War Cabinet was aware that the Roosevelt administration was "acutely uneasy" lest the British start the "Japanese eyeing the Netherlands East Indies." In fact, Lord Lothian had advised Churchill that the scare tactics were working, citing recent actions had "provoked fear...lest the East Indies provide [a] back door for America's entrance into the European war...."[268]

The insights provided by the British ambassador to the United States of June 21 and 22, after France's demise, are illustrative:

> The essential line to be taken in England is to stress our determination to fight Germany, our conviction that if we repel the impending German attack the tide will have turned toward victory, and that assistance which the US can give in the next weeks and months may make the difference between victory and defeat.
>
> Our stand on the Burma Road probably brings us more in the way of increased belief in our resolution than in augmenting the possibility of effective US cooperation in the Far East.[269]

Another example of these rather isolated indications of the British policy to avoid making peace by way of convincing the US that her vital interests were at stake can be found in a private circular for the members of the British House of Lords and Commons, entitled "The Consequences of the French Defeat for Britain."

> Those who state that "we can't trust Hitler" should remember what we are now doing with Russia and even our efforts with Japan.[270]

A Four-Point Plan to Avoid a Premature Peace

The memorandum's mention of "Russia" is certainly not inconsequential. It refers to Sir Stafford Cripps's most recent visit to Moscow. Could it be that the real intent of the Cripps mission was more than simply the settling of economic questions? The British government knew of Stalin's dismay over the quick demise of France, and wanted to assure the Soviet leadership that the present British government intended to fight on, but they could not predict the future with any certainty—some future government might be forced to sue for peace after succumbing to a German invasion. The British government intended to sow the seeds of fear. They wanted Stalin to mull over the prospects. If Britain were pacified, Hitler would finally have a free hand to do what he had always wanted to do in the first place—smash the "Bolshevik threat" and establish German "Lebensraum" at the expense of the USSR. Churchill felt that he had to sow the seeds of fear in Stalin to avoid making a premature peace with Hitler. He had to convince the Soviets that a German invasion of Britain was *imminent*, while at the same time convincing the members of his own inner circle that such an invasion was *not* pending.

The British were engaged in a general policy of this sort for the consumption of the whole world, and Churchill sought specifically to convince Washington and Moscow of four certainties—even though the Prime Minister did not really believe that all were inevitable:

1. That France was doomed without US or Soviet intervention.

2. That, with the fall of France, a successful German invasion of Britain was on the near horizon.

3. That Britain was determined, against all odds, to fight on alone.

4. That the ultimate consequence of German victory, whether it came by way of military force or by a negotiated peace, would put the vital interests of the US and Soviet Union in jeopardy.

If Washington and Moscow could be convinced of these future "certainties," Britain stood a much better chance of avoiding armistice with Nazi Germany. At least one of Churchill's "four fears" was accurate.

Desperate Calls and Maneuverings

The events of the first weeks of June on the battlefield made the fall of France inevitable.

On June 6, 1940, the French premier, Paul Reynaud, telephoned Roosevelt and attempted to convince the President that if the US did not intervene militarily in the near future, the future of France was at stake. Even though it appeared at the time that Paris was in danger, Roosevelt replied that he would only "go as far as the law would permit and even a little further to help him."[271] So, FDR would covertly aid the Allies, but he was not able to render direct military assistance.

No desperate call to the Soviets was necessary to provoke Stalin to action. Since the fall of France was expected, and an end to the war in the west appeared imminent, Stalin acted with alacrity to put his nation in the best strategic position to handle any contingency. By June 15, the Soviets had moved a number of divisions into the Baltic region. By the end of June, Stalin's armies had moved into Romania, to reclaim the regions known as Bessarabia and North Bukovina—a move that put a hefty Soviet strike force within an hour's march of Romania's rich oil region.

Back on the western front, the war was winding down. On June 14, Churchill and Halifax had flown out to meet Reynaud in Tours in order to bolster the French government and "to dissuade him from giving up."[272] All that really came of this dramatic meeting was Reynaud's decision to once again telephone Roosevelt, a communication intercepted by the German "B Dienst" (the code-breaking service) and deciphered. In fact, Goebbels, the German propaganda chief, was privy to the content of this cable within two days. He relates in his diary of June 16, 1940, that "Roosevelt cables Reynaud: as much material aid as possible. And America will not recognize any theft of French territory."[273]

Roosevelt's reply must have dashed the hopes of the French leadership, for even as Churchill was cabling Roosevelt on June 16, about the inevitability of the British Isles "becoming a vassal state of the Hitler Empire," the French were putting out peace feelers—claiming that the French government desired a full hearing of Germany's conditions for an armistice.[274]

President Roosevelt first learned of this tragic development by way of Anthony Biddle, who had immediately telegrammed the US Secretary of State with this simple message: "Pétain and a peace cabinet have succeeded Reynaud."[275]

Biddle sent another "Triple Priority" telegram to Cordell Hull, explaining in greater detail what had transpired. Paul Baudoin, the new French foreign minister, had informed him at midnight on June 16 that the new Pétain government had requested the services of the Spanish government to act as an intermediary. The Spanish were asked to find out from the German government on what terms an armistice would be granted. The initial communication went through the Spanish ambassador to France.

Baudoin "formally assured" Biddle, who, in turn, notified the US Secretary of State, that the French fleet "would never be surrendered to Germany," as guaranteed by Admiral Darlan, who had been "named Minister of Marine" in Pétain's government.

Desperate Measures

On the British side, a last-minute attempt to destroy the validity of the new French government, by proposing a political union between the two nations failed miserably.

Churchill was forced to "allow" France to renege on its covenant with Britain, never to sign a separate armistice or peace.[276] When the French government asked Churchill to graciously let France out of that promise, the British Prime Minister replied that he would be willing, on one condition—that the French either scuttle or turn their navy over to the British immediately.[277]

At this proclamation, the French balked angrily. The new French government was livid. At that time, the Germans had not even made a demand upon France to turn over the fleet. Moreover, the French felt betrayed by the British, who had consistently encouraged the French to fight on against all odds, while they themselves escaped across the channel to safety. It seemed that the British government had unnecessarily spilled French blood just to save the British Armies at Dunkirk from having to surrender. During the critical days of the French army's retreat Churchill had also recalled the Spitfires to the safety of airbases in England, exposing the French army to aerial bombardment.

The French could not understand Churchill's demand for the fleet in particular. Until it was clear that Hitler was demanding the fleet as a term of an armistice, how dare the Prime Minister make the demand *himself*! The French understood the threat that German possession of the French fleet would pose to the British Isles and Empire. If it had been a German demand, the Pétain government recognized that such a British *request*, not *demand*, would be reasonable. Churchill's demand could go unheeded until the Germans had made the demand. In the end, no such demand on the part of the Germans was ever made. Therefore, the French, especially Admiral Darlan, considered Churchill's demand to be utterly groundless.

More puzzling was that this British demand did not go away, even after it was clear that the armistice between Germany and France did not include the handing over of the French fleet. The whole world looked on in amazement as Britain's demands upon France began to take on a warlike tone.

In Washington, Roosevelt was busy trying to keep the British and new French governments on friendly terms.[278] However, British actions directly militated against the President's efforts.

Armistice Terms

Hitler had completely understood the necessity of not imposing crushing terms on the French.[279] Although Hitler was advised by his admirals that the confiscation of the French fleet would greatly increase the chances of success in an invasion of Britain, the dictator was not thinking in terms of continuing the struggle. He wanted to come to terms with Britain and to end the war.

The first sign of this "surprisingly conciliatory" attitude was already evident on June 17, at Hitler and Mussolini's meeting at the Munich Führer Building. At the meeting, Mussolini posed the question of what should be done with the French navy, inserting that perhaps the Axis partners should demand that it be handed over as a part of the armistice conditions. To this proposal, Hitler retorted that he was not in favor of subjecting the French to harsh conditions, and that he was dead-set opposed to the notion of making a demand for the French navy, citing that "If we make the demand...the whole French fleet will go over to the British." As it turns out, a primary result of this meeting of the dictators was the issuance of a "solemn declaration" to the French government that Germany "does not intend to make any demands on the French fleet," and Hitler's expression to Mussolini that he felt that it would not be a good thing to destroy the British Empire.[280]

To Field Marshal Keitel fell the task of working up an armistice draft. The entire document was Keitel's creation and met with Hitler's approval, with the exception of the preamble—Hitler reserved the writing of the document's introduction for himself.[281]

Here is the pertinent section of the Franco-German armistice, regarding the disposition of the French fleet from Article VIII:

The French war fleet is to collect in ports to be designated more particularly, and under German and/or Italian control to demobilize and lay up with the exception of those units released to the French Government for protection of French interests in its colonial empire.

The peacetime stations of ships should control the designation of ports.

The German Government solemnly declares to the French Government that it does not intend to use the French War Fleet, which is in harbors under German control for its purposes in war, with the exception of units necessary for the purposes of guarding the coast and sweeping mines.

It further solemnly and expressly declares that it does not intend to bring up any demands respecting the French War Fleet at the conclusion of a peace.

All warships outside France are to be recalled to France with the exception of that portion of the French War Fleet which shall be designated to represent French interests in the colonial empire.[282]

Since Mussolini had entered the war on June 10, 1940, in order to get in on the French spoils of war, an armistice was also signed between the Pétain government and Italy. In articles 6 and 12 of the Franco-Italian armistice the wording is nearly identical to the Franco-German armistice in respect to the disposition of the French fleet. The agreement was signed by the head of the French delegation, Huntziger, and the chief of the Italian armed forces, Badoglio, on June 24, 1940, at Villa Incisa, some 12 miles north of Rome.[283]

Then what of Churchill's decision to use the British navy to attack the French fleet at Dakar, Oran, Alexandria, and Mers-el-kebir? Churchill was well informed on the German intentions concerning the French fleet. He knew that the Germans would not demand, and were not demanding, the handing over of the French navy as an armistice condition. So why did Churchill attack the French fleet?

At Mers-el-kebir, a British attack resulted when the French admiral in charge failed to submit to a British ultimatum to surrender and consent to a British navy boarding party. This refusal led to a savage attack by the British navy and R.A.F.—an attack which killed 1,000 Frenchmen![284] The US government was mystified at the time as to what Churchill was doing. Did he want to drive the Pétain government to Hitler's side?

We Mean to Fight!

US Secretary of State Cordell Hull relates in his account of these incidents that when Churchill later came to Washington in December of 1941, the Prime Minister finally explained his decision to attack the French fleet with these words:

> Many people throughout the world believed that Britain was about ready to surrender [and, I] had wanted by this action to show that she [Britain] meant to fight.[285]

110

Secretary Hull makes it seem that he was not aware of Churchill's reasoning, *at the time of the attack*. However, there may be good reason to doubt this interpretation. There is, of course, no doubt that Churchill risked driving the Vichy French government into Hitler's arms. At the same time, there is also no doubt that the US government would have ceased its aid to Britain immediately if Roosevelt felt that Britain was about to capitulate.[286]

British Ambassador to the US Lothian sent a military report on July 4, to Roosevelt, which contains some intriguing handwritten postscript on the issue of British attacks on the French navy. At the bottom of the document, Lothian points out to the President that he "will see that Winston Churchill has taken the action in regard to the French fleet which we discussed and you approved."[287] Incredibly, it seems that FDR had suggested the attack. At the very least, it is safe to conclude that the American President was fully aware of, and agreed with, Churchill's reasoning for the attacks.

The Roosevelt administration vigorously sought to do everything in its power, short of actual participation, to help the British now that France had been beaten. But there must have been more than just continued US shipments and Roosevelt's words sustaining Churchill's confidence. He seems so confident that Britain did not have its back up to the wall, and could therefore avoid coming to terms with Hitler, that he could risk losing France to the Axis. That is some kind of confidence.

Curious Developments

Perhaps the British Prime Minister saw the Soviet occupation of Kaunas and Vilna on June 15 and the installment of a new Lithuanian puppet government on June 16 as a sign that he could hold out—and the longer the better. These developments were indications to Churchill that although his nation was, now standing alone, it might not be for much longer. Similar Soviet demands on Estonia and Latvia were made for Soviet troop access to their territories. These ultimatums were conceded to on June 20 and 22.

Yet another positive indication from the United States government helped to *sustain* Churchill's position of intransigence. This development helped to make his government less vulnerable to a German peace offensive, on the same day that the USSR made their demands upon Estonia and Latvia. President Roosevelt had proposed to reorganize his cabinet—nominating two prominent Republican statesmen, Stimson for Secretary of State for War and Knox for Secretary of the Navy. Why did this cause celebration in London? The answer is that the inclusion of the opposition party in such key positions was uniformly the step taken in parliamentary democracies when forming a *War Cabinet*. FDR appeared to be gearing up for war-readiness.[288] Despite this encouraging news, not every development coming out of the US was rosy.

An American journalist, Karl von Wiegand, interviewed Hitler after the capitulation of France. In the interview, which was widely published in the US, Hitler claimed that he wanted an end to the war, that he did not want war with Britain, and that he had absolutely no designs on the western hemisphere. Churchill was relieved to hear from his eyes and ears in Washington, Lothian, that "Wiegand's interview…was received by all from the President downwards with polite or open derision."[289]

The President of the United States had good reason to believe that Britain could avoid making a hasty peace with Hitler because of what he knew about Soviet developments. Roosevelt was keenly aware of the Soviet fear of a possible "western crusade" against Bolshevism and how that belief made Stalin rather susceptible to a change in policy. The Soviet leadership was having an anxiety attack of such great proportions that the news of Soviet displeasure with Germany's stunning victory came streaming into Washington from Soviet sources as diverse as Latvia, China, Romania, and Morocco. A cable received from the US minister to Latvia, John C. Wiley, is perhaps most insightful, for it highlights the Soviet fear of a *western conspiracy*. Wiley reported to the American Secretary of State that the Kremlin was "in a state of acute anxiety," especially over "Hitler's recent statements—that he did not desire the destruction of the British Empire." According to Wiley, the Soviet leadership feared "that the problems of western Europe would be solved at Russia's expense."[290]

Not unrelated to this information relayed through an American source was the visit of Sir Stafford Cripps to Moscow. Cripps' mission was to sow the seeds of fear in Moscow, as has been previously mentioned. The German ambassador to the USSR, Schulenberg, was assigned the task of reporting to the German Foreign Office and Foreign Ministry on the developments related to Cripps' mission. Schulenberg reported to the Foreign Office "England was daily expecting a sudden attack [which] would very likely be successful." To underline the fact that Cripps was towing a Churchill line, when the Swedish minister in Moscow asked Cripps, "Why then did not Britain make peace?" Cripps responded that Britain could not, because Germany would call for the "surrender of the entire British fleet."[291] This, of course, was a total falsehood and is obviously right out of the Churchill playbook. It was the same scare tactic used by Churchill to make the "handing over of the French fleet" loom as a greater threat than it actually was. Now, the brilliant Prime Minister used the same ploy to sow anxiety in Moscow.

Hitler's Delusion

At this juncture it is important to come to grips with what the German government's thoughts were in the context of France's capitulation and the emergence of a mood of intransigence on the part of the US and USSR. After all, the Soviet government had, at the time of the defeat of Poland, readily offered its services as a mediator to end the war and publicly proclaimed its desire to see the war come to an end. Now, no such proclamations were forthcoming.

If Churchill was busy sowing the seeds of intransigence abroad in order to avoid making peace with Hitler, then what should be made of the peace feelers emanating from Britain at that time?

Goebbels reports in his diary on June 25 that Hitler "Believes that the [British] Empire must be preserved if at all possible" and further confided "negotiations are already under way...via Sweden for example."[292] Goebbels' understudy, Willi A. Boelke, wrote of reports of British peace feelers in his log of Propaganda Ministry conferences. What was the source of these peace feelers? Following up on Goebbels' reference to "Sweden" seemed like a good place to start.

Fransoni, the Italian minister in Stockholm, likewise reported to the Italian Foreign Ministry that the British government was ready "to discuss peace." According to this source, the good offices of the Swedish foreign minister had been requested to help bring about an end to the war.[293] Word also reached the German Foreign Office and Foreign Ministry around the same time, by way of the Swedish foreign minister, that in Britain "no opportunity would be neglected for concluding a compromise peace if the chance is offered on reasonable conditions" and that British "die-hards" could not "stand in the way."[294] The Swedish foreign minister revealed the source of this peace feeler as being R.A. Butler of the British Foreign Office.

With reports of this sort coming in, the German government had some ray of hope that the war could be brought to an end. A cautious optimism took root in the German government. Once again, before these sources could be verified, Ribbentrop did not want news leaking out to the press prematurely. This would have undermined German morale if the reports turned out to be false, since similar reports had usually turned out to be lacking in real substance.

Weizsäcker, at the German Foreign Office, similarly notes in his memoirs that the reports were coming in from England, which "seemed to indicate that we might expect the British to come some way to meet us." There were rumors of peace during the first weeks of July 1940, and Hitler would have liked to exit the war with Britain. Hitler was encouraged by these feelers, and perhaps led on by them. Hitler "wanted an understanding with England," and had "postponed his planned Reichstag speech again and again in order to give England time and room enough to make the hoped-for decision to ask for terms." The Führer was perplexed as to why the British were remaining intransigent and concluded that Churchill was blocking the road to negotiations. Hitler concluded that the British Prime Minister's ability to hold his ground was somehow attached to recent British dealings with Roosevelt and Stalin.[295] Hitler's intuition was right on target. Nevertheless, it did not stop Hitler from holding on to the idea of negotiating a peace with Britain. He openly shared his hope with nearly all of the top members of the German government, the vast majority of whom shared Hitler's opinion.

According to Felix Kersten's memoirs, the SS underling had had a conversation with Rudolf Hess on June 24, 1940. Hess related that Hitler wanted peace, saying, "We'll make peace with England," and insisting that he knew that Hitler had "allowed the English Army to escape at Dunkirk" as a face-saving gesture. Hess waxed almost poetic as he told Kersten of the dawning of a new era of "fruitful Franco-German cooperation." Hess "fantasized about how France, England, and Germany would soon unite in peace and stand together against the Bolshevik threat."[296]

An extremely unusual reference by Weizsäcker in his war remembrances is made regarding peace feelers emanating from "Lord Lothian" in Washington. The reference is strange because it occurred around the same time that Lothian was sharing with US Secretary of State Hull, "Britain's belief," based on information gained in Moscow by Cripps and by the Soviet ambassador in London, Maisky, that "Russia" might cease to "assist" Hitler.[297] It is obvious that the information in this case came by way of Sir Stafford Cripps, because the word "assist" was so often used in his conversations with Churchill and the War Cabinet when referring to the schemes afoot to halt Soviet economic aid to Germany. Lothian peace feelers have the distinct feel of a *disinformation campaign* about them, considering Lothian's place in Churchill's ploy to scare the Americans into the war. It is not at all clear, though, that the German government picked up on this possibility. Hitler would have to put aside his uncertainties about the possible duplicity of such leads if he was to get the British to come to terms. Following up on feelers was not enough for Hitler. He decided that he would wait a bit longer, and then make his desire for peace abundantly clear to the world in a Reichstag address. As he planned the content and wording of this speech, the German dictator did so with the possibility of a Soviet about-face lurking in the darkest recesses of his mind.[298]

The Chief of the German General Staff, Keitel, provides the following insight regarding Hitler's mindset at the time in his memoirs:

But above all he [Hitler] was reluctant to countenance the inevitable loss of his last chance of settling the war with Britain by diplomatic means.[299]

In General Leeb's diary of June 2, 1940, one finds a similar account:

He [Hitler] points out that without a navy the equal of Britain's we [Germany] could not hold on to her colonies for long. Thus, we can easily find a basis for a peace agreement with Britain."[300]

Hitler's thoughts of coming to terms with Britain can be established as far back as June 10, 1940, during the campaign in France. In the papers of Walther Hewel, one can find the original draft of an official statement regarding Italy's entrance into the war on Germany's side. The first draft that was sent for Hitler's approval read:

German and Italian soldiers will now march shoulder to shoulder and not rest until Britain and France have been beaten.[301]

On Hitler's amended version of the announcement, he scratched out "Britain." Already, Hitler was looking to engineer a British climb-down by helping her to save face.

On the day that Pétain's government was created, Hitler had told General von Rundstedt that:

Now that Britain will presumably be willing to make peace, I will begin the final settlement of scores with bolshevism.[302]

Even earlier, in late May 1940, Hitler had predicted to von Rundstedt that:

In six weeks there would be peace and he would make a gentleman's peace with England.[303]

Hitler's racism played a major part in fostering what in many ways was nothing less than a delusion. For example, Hitler told General Alfred Jodl's principal assistant on June 17, 1940, that he did not intend to destroy the British Empire. To the contrary, the destruction of Britain would be a blow to the white race.[304]

Jodl's diary includes an even earlier reference of this sort. On May 20, 1940, he wrote about how Hitler was "beside himself with joy" over the rapid progress of the German forces in France. Jodl's diary shows that Hitler's mind was already racing ahead. He recorded that Hitler was "working on a peace treaty [for France]" and that "Britain can get a separate peace any time after restitution of the colonies [Germany's]."[305]

One of the most important staff officers of the German army high command, Major Leyhle, told General Blumentritt during May and June of 1940 that the Führer had "often talked to him about the idea of coming to an agreement with England."[306]

Halder's war diary contains a commentary on what he heard Hitler say at a meeting of the German general staff on July 13, 1940:

[Hitler] accepts that he may have to force Britain to make peace; but is reluctant to do so, because if we do defeat the British in the field, the British Empire will fall apart. Germany will not profit therefrom. We should be paying with German blood for something from which only Japan, America, and others would draw benefit.[307]

Peace with Britain was a real hope for Hitler. Others who, perhaps, saw things more realistically were pressing Hitler to get on with war plans against Britain. Hitler found himself in the unusual position of being under intense pressure from the German War Office to launch a cross-channel invasion against Britain. This was the same group of generals who had been reluctant to the point of treason when it came to the decision to invade Poland and launch an offensive against France in November of 1939! Now, Hitler was resisting *their* war formulations.

Hitler had grave misgivings about the general staff's proposed plan for an invasion of Britain. He was particularly concerned that the German navy could not provide adequate security for a cross-channel invasion.[308] As time went on and Britain was not coming around, Hitler did throw himself into the minutia of the plan, demanding the most innovative preparations and every improvisation in order to speed preparations. However, according to Hitler's leading military advisor, his heart was not really in it.

Field Marshal Keitel puts it this way in his memoirs:

I also had the feeling that not only was Hitler appalled by the thought of the senseless loss of human life a failure would entail, but above all he was reluctant to countenance the inevitable loss of his last chance of settling the war with Britain by diplomatic means—something which I am convinced he was at that time still hoping to achieve.[309]

Hitler, according to Keitel, was already worried about what Stalin's intentions were in late June and July of 1940, because the Soviets had occupied the

Baltic nations, parts of Romania, and had moved up a massive force to the German-Soviet frontier during the French campaign. Hitler wondered whether he could risk putting so much of his essential forces on the line for such a risky venture against England, while the Soviets seemed poised to strike.[310] Could Hitler be certain that Stalin would not take advantage of Germany's necessarily weak defenses in the east, while a cross-channel invasion was under way?

Keitel claims that the German War Office did everything in its power to promote the execution of Operation Sea Lion. By all accounts, Hitler resisted this pressure, sometimes directly, usually in a passive-aggressive way. Hitler was inclined to give Britain "one last chance of getting off comparatively easy."[311]

In addition to Hitler's personal desire to end the war with Britain, he really had some reason to believe that Britain might come to terms with Germany. His hopes were sustained by more than just some unrealistic, racist fantasies.

Any Brits for a Settlement?

Pope Pius XII had made an urgent plea for the belligerents to come to terms on July 2. Dino Alfieri, the Italian ambassador to Berlin, was busy attempting to draw the United States into placing pressure on the British government to come to terms with Hitler—stressing to FDR that neither of the Axis partners wanted the destruction of England, let alone war with England.[312] Furthermore, Hitler could never be certain of Churchill's ability to stay in power, being keenly aware of the desires for peace among some of the highest-placed British statesmen.

Were there really high-ranking members of the British government who would have negotiated with Hitler, or was Hitler just being led on by Churchill, who just wanted to use the fact that he knew Hitler wanted to end the war in order to gain more time?

Sir Henry Channon was certainly an example of a high-ranking British statesman. Channon was a staunch supporter of Chamberlain and hoped for his political resurgence—at Churchill's expense. On the day that Chamberlain was hospitalized, Channon wearily wrote, "thus fades the last hope of peace" in his diary.[313] He had always regarded Churchill as a warmonger and blamed him and his political Allies for destroying Chamberlain's prewar foreign policy as well as Chamberlain's Peace Front strategy during the long months of the Phony War. Remarkably, Channon was not completely correct about Churchill.

Evidence that has surfaced in recent years indicates that even Churchill considered an armistice with Germany after the fall of France, if he could be convinced that Hitler would make a tolerable offer. At the time of the Franco-German armistice, Churchill had put it this way to his cabinet members:

> If Herr Hitler was prepared to make peace on the terms of the restoration of German colonies and the overlordship of Central Europe, that was one thing. But it is quite unlikely that he would make any such offer.[314]

Churchill went on to say that he would not ask for terms. He would not *condescend* to do what the French had done. He *was*, on the other hand, ready to consider an armistice if Germany made the approach.[315] He wanted to avoid looking like the supplicant, because he felt that *Britain* had not been beaten.

It is necessary to draw back from Churchill's rather monolithic claim that the British government "never for a moment considered peace." There is truth in his claim, but its veracity rests on a technicality of sorts.

There is no doubt that Churchill was an intrepid leader. There is no doubt that he was working with every ounce of energy to avoid making a premature peace with Hitler. However, even before the French were defeated, the British War Cabinet minutes establish that he *did* put the idea on the table for serious and open debate.

During the darkest days of the tenuous Dunkirk evacuation, Churchill notified the War Cabinet that he was willing to countenance the notion of negotiations with Nazi Germany. Neville Chamberlain's diary confirms what has been found in the War Cabinet minutes. The notes of the May 26, 1940, meeting reveals his suggestion "that he would be thankful to get out of our present difficulties, provided we retained the essentials of our vital strength, even at the cost of some cession of territory."[316]

What exactly was Churchill referring to, regarding territorial concessions? It would make sense that his comment was about finally giving up on the demand the British government had been making about returning Czechoslovakia and Poland to their pre-1939 boundaries. It would also make sense for Churchill to be considering the idea of granting Germany the colonies that had been stripped from her by the Versailles Treaty. As it turns out, the Prime Minister made reference to neither option. Neville Chamberlain's personal summary of the War Cabinet meetings of May 27, 1940, contains these words:

> if we could get out of this jam by giving up Malta and Gibraltar and some African colonies he [Churchill] would jump at it.

At first blush, it seems as if Churchill is talking about getting out of the war. Most historians who have dealt with this curious phrase have concluded as much. Consideration of the particular words, within the general context of the British government's desire to keep Italy out of the war, lends itself to a different interpretation. The ceding of Malta, Gibraltar and some African colonies would be appealing to *Italy*, not so much Germany. It must be remembered that Italy, on May 27, had not yet entered the fray—and that the British government was doing everything it could to keep Italy out. Keeping Italy out of the war was necessary to sustain the French in their death throes. It is not surprising in the least that Churchill considered *buying Italy off*, so to speak.

What is *true* about Churchill's claim that his government *never considered* peace with Hitler is a matter of *timing*. During the first two and a half weeks of July, his government *did not* consider terms, simply because Germany had not yet forwarded any specific terms. During the period from June 16, 1940, and roughly the end of the second week of July 1940, the German government was mulling over the peace feelers coming in from many sources, including *unofficial* British sources. Hitler waited to develop a fuller picture of his chances for peace. He was waiting to gather all possible evidence to use, if it was once again going to be up to him to make a public declaration. At the same time, according to the British War Cabinet minutes, Churchill had decided to consider peace proposals only when offered by Germany.

Churchill held his internal critics, FDR, and Stalin at bay by fostering the image of the inevitability of a German invasion and/or extremely harsh terms, when he knew that to be untrue. He did this precisely because it was the best way he could think of to *avoid* coming to the peace table with Hitler.

The Churchill government had been vulnerable early on in the desperate and confusing days following France's capitulation. With every passing day, that "inevitable" German attack on England was dissipating. By the time that Hitler made his grandiose appeal for peace on July 19, 1940, Churchill and his inner circle knew that no real invasion was coming. If Hitler had made his appeal two weeks earlier, chances of success would have been far better. Once again, Hitler had delayed his official proposal in order to gather vital intelligence information on the Churchill government. He thought that it would be necessary to discredit Churchill in particular in order to make way for new leadership in Britain—leaders willing to deal. He could not resist the chance to do unto Churchill what had been done unto him back in October of 1939—when the British government had upped the ante for peace by saying they would no longer negotiate with the "Hitler regime." It had all become very personal to the German dictator. To him, *Churchill* was the "warmonger."

Hitler had delayed his peace address in order to incorporate what he thought would be regarded as "damning" evidence against Churchill. Hitler was made aware of the broad outline of the evidence in late June but did not have the full translation of the documents he planned to incorporate into his speech to besmirch Churchill until July 5. On that day, some very important information gained by the German Foreign Ministry was made public by Ribbentrop. The foreign minister had convinced Hitler to delay his address again until some additional Allied documents discovered by a German soldier in La Charité were translated and made public. Hitler felt that these documents, in particular, represented the "diplomatic revolution" necessary to convince those members of the British government who were suppressed by Churchill to push the Prime Minister aside.

By some bolt of luck a hapless German soldier on duty in La Charité, France, had found some top-secret documents of the Allied Supreme War Council, replete with marginal notes in the original handwriting of Gamelin, Daladier, Weygand, Churchill, and others. The secret documents included the plan to "switch the war to Scandinavia," the Allied scheme to start a conflagration or possible front of attrition in the Balkans, and a plan to use Turkish aerodromes to bomb the Soviet oil-producing districts of the Caucasus.[317] On July 5, the German Foreign Office published White Book No. 6, which was a collection of the above-mentioned Allied war planning documents of February through April of 1940. German newspapers ran articles based on the various tid-bits from these captured documents. By July 6, the information was appearing in newspapers all over the globe; including the *New York Times*, the *London Times*, and the official Soviet paper *Izvestia*.

It was not just for the sake of providing time for the information to prepare the ground for his speech that it was delayed. Additionally, some intemperate comments made by Sir Stafford Cripps, the British special envoy to Moscow, had also come to Hitler's attention on July 5—more words that Hitler could use to smear Churchill as "warmonger." Cripps had told the Swedish ambassador in Moscow that in the case of a successful German invasion of England that Churchill would escape with his government to Canada and fight on from there.[318] Hitler was delighted to hear that Churchill could be made to look like a warmonger, coward, and abandoner of his own people—this had to be played up in the speech as much as possible.

Outside events also worked to delay Hitler's speech. Europe was again in the throes of diplomatic and political realignment, and Hitler felt that he needed to get a grip on the ramifications of these events in order to construct his speech. He had to consider the sensibilities of all the parties involved while using these new developments to spin Britain's position as being untenable and increasingly isolated.

In Romania a new cabinet had been formed, with Girgurtu as Prime Minister. Girgurtu was a member of Romania's fascist Iron Guard. This new Romanian government was pro-German. It now proclaimed its intentions to adhere to the "Axis system." In France, Marshal Pétain broke off diplomatic relations with Britain because of the afore-mentioned attacks on the French navy. The Vichy French government was on the verge of declaring war on Britain.[319]

From the beginning of July, it seems that nearly every French official with even limited access to the German government was lobbying for a new understanding with Hitler's Germany. They wanted to step beyond the armistice agreement and work out a far-reaching peace settlement. Vichy Foreign Minister Paul Baudouin was tasked by Pétain to arrange a face-to-face meeting with Ribbentrop. The intent of this meeting was to propose that France become an "associated power."[320] General Huntziger, the Frenchman whose signature can be found on the Franco-German and Franco-Italian armistices, was a leading proponent of taking the next step in creating a new relationship between France and Germany.[321] The French were aghast at British attacks on the French navy and efforts to undermine the French colonial empire, when France was at its weakest point.

The French had an armistice with Germany. They now desired an official peace treaty. The Vichy government of Pétain wanted an end to German occupation, and the German government expressed its desire to oblige. However, as long as a state of war existed between Britain and Germany, Germany could not possibly consent to a withdrawal, lest the British make fresh landings in France. Pétain understood the dilemma and suggested to the German government that perhaps the best way to end the war was to present Britain with a united front for peace between France and Germany. In pursuit of this goal, the Pétain government requested that Hitler give them more flexibility in responding to British encroachment on French colonial possessions. Hitler's response was to grant the Vichy French government the right to use its navy to defend its interests abroad. The Pétain administration and Hitler agreed that allowing the French to escape certain restrictions imposed by the armistice, France could move to defend itself. Moreover, if France could defend its interest and present a united front for peace with Germany, then the British were more likely to climb down and come to the peace table.[322]

Hitler, Ribbentrop, and Ciano met at the Chancellery building in Berlin on July 6, 1940. At this meeting Hitler announced his intention to "make a very magnanimous peace offer to England" to his Italian ally.[323] Even the usually pessimistic Italian foreign minister "behaved as if the war was already over."[324]

It seemed to Hitler that as time went on, in July 1940, circumstances in Europe were piling up in his favor. All of the events seemed to be setting him up to achieve his goal of getting Britain to come to terms.

Hitler had "astonished" his general staff back in late May, when the war was not even over yet in France, by

> speaking with admiration of the British Empire, of the civilization that Britain had brought into the world....He said that all he wanted from Britain was that she should acknowledge Germany's position on the continent....He concluded by saying that his aim was to make peace with Britain on a basis that she would regard as compatible with her honor to accept.[325]

Since Hitler was convinced that only "Churchill and his clique" stood in the way of a reasonable arrangement, it was decided that the official line to be taken up in the German press and radio addresses to England was to "attack Churchill" and *not* the British people.

On July 9, Goebbels explained to his staff at the Propaganda Ministry that the current line of personal attacks was based on the German government's desire to avoid the "annihilation" of Britain, and that the government's official position was that Britain "should be given one last chance of getting off comparatively easy."[326] At the same time, the German Foreign Office became party to the propaganda machine by sending out official and unofficial peace feelers to prepare the world for Hitler's speech.

On July 12, Ribbentrop's office received the news from Madrid that Franco was willing to serve as a go-between to end the war. General Franco took the position that Britain "had lost the war" but was willing to "serve England" in order to affect a fair peace.[327] The German, Italian and French governments all announced that they welcomed the effort, while the British government announced that Franco's efforts were "premature" and suggested that the Spanish head of state was biased. Despite this rejection, Franco then sought, through diplomatic back channels, to find out what Hitler's terms were. The German Foreign Office was instructed to respond that Hitler would soon make his terms abundantly clear in an up and coming grand speech.

Regarding the contents of Hitler's address, he kept it close to the vest. Few individuals knew the specific details of the speech. Many of the highest-ranking officials in the German government were a bit miffed about the fact too. They wanted to be able to facilitate the effectiveness of the speech if at all possible. To do so would require more inside information than Hitler was comfortable allowing. He feared that any premature leaks of his speech's contents would just give Churchill time to figure out some clever ploy to destroy its effectiveness. Hitler felt that he had learned from his last grand peace speech that had been solidly rejected. The last time he had *purposefully* leaked the proposals.

Many in the German government were left to speculate. Goebbels, for instance, guessed that the speech's primary purpose was to gain peace by provoking a Churchill resignation.[328] Even Hitler's second in command, Hermann Göring knew that "Hitler still hoped for reconciliation" with Britain and expected Hitler to say so in the speech, but he had not been permitted to review the text—even though he had asked Hitler to review it personally, claiming that he needed to know the contents in order to make pertinent transitional statements. The Reichsmarschall was to introduce Hitler, after all.

Göring revealed in his postwar interrogations that, as far as he knew, no one advised Hitler on the speech or on British foreign affairs at the time "except Ribbentrop."[329]

Göring's statement after the war to his American interrogators does at least fit the context, since Hitler's speech had been delayed in order to make use of the captured Allied documents. These documents were brought to Hitler's attention by Ribbentrop. Indeed, if one surveys a passage from Hitler's Reichstag address, one cannot help but notice the German foreign minister's influence:

with the intention of appealing once more and for the last time to common sense....Even on September 2, as Mussolini made his peace proposal, I agreed, but the Anglo-French warmongers wanted war to be continued....On June 19, 1940, a German soldier found a curious document....They were the secret documents of the Allied Supreme War Council, and included the minutes of every meeting held by this illustrious body. This time Mr. Churchill will not succeed in contesting the veracity of these documents...these...bear marginal notes written by Gamelin, Daladier, Weygand...[who]...attempted to use Finland in their own interests, they were determined to turn Norway and Sweden into a theater of war, that they planned a conflagration in the Balkans in order to gain the assistance of 100 divisions in those countries....Then on October 6, 1939, I addressed the German people....I appealed to the heads of the enemy states....For this peaceful proposition of mine I was abused. Mr. Chamberlain spat upon me in the eyes of the world....In order to secure Norwegian and Swedish ore the British were going to land in Norway and march into Sweden....Only a few weeks ago Mr. Churchill said he wanted war....I am not the vanquished begging for mercy. I speak as a victor. I can see no reason why this war must go on. We should like to avert the sacrifices which must claim millions....It is possible that Mr. Churchill will once again brush aside this statement of mine by saying that it is merely born out of fear and doubt of victory. In that case I shall have relieved my conscience of the things to come.[330]

The entire speech was broadcast all over the world by the German Foreign Language Services, and Hitler's personal interpreter, Paul Schmidt, was given the specific task by Hitler to make sure that the English version was read with absolute clarity and precision. Schmidt had been instructed by Ribbentrop to "stress as much as possible points which might appeal to the other side."[331]

Hitler's address of July 19, 1940, was not just an appeal to Britain. It was a victory oration. Commendations and promotions were bestowed upon nearly all of the various heads of the German armed forces on an unprecedented scale. Its contents were not dominated by specific peace proposals. The speech does not reveal an attempt to repeat his desire for peace in an emphatic fashion, although it was placed at the climax of the address. The tone and mood of the speech was not bombastic or strident. It was not a typical Hitler war speech. By the same token, he did not go out of his way to sound conciliatory. Rather, he attacked Churchill. According to the diary of Sir Henry Channon, he and "Rab" Butler had switched on the radio to listen to the speech, "but it was so badly relayed that [they] understood little except that he seemed less ranting and less hysterical than usual."[332] American journalist William L. Shirer attended the speech and was impressed by Hitler's ability to pull off the perfect mixture of the "confidence of the conqueror" and the "humbleness" that plays so well with the public when "they know a man is on top."[333] Shirer, who was there firsthand, as well as anyone who simply reads the text, cannot escape the impression that something was missing.

Hitler's call for an end to the war *did not contain any specific proposals*. It is not entirely discernable why. Again, this is partially due to the fact that he did not share his thinking on the speech's development with anyone outside of Ribbentrop, and Ribbentrop's memoirs do not contribute anything of additional significance on the matter.

It would have made sense for Hitler's address to include at least some specifics, indicative of just how *light* his terms for peace actually were. On the other side of the coin, it could be argued that the absence of any specifics indicated that there were no preconditions. Perhaps Hitler intended his offer to be open-ended so as not to prejudice any special-interest group in Britain.

The absence of specifics could very well have been Hitler's attempt to indicate a "no strings attached" attitude.

The absence of particulars in Hitler's offer may have also been due to his lack of confidence in being able to "get through" to the "English mentality." There is some evidence suggestive of such an interpretation. Hitler may have written the speech with a mind full of doubt. Specifics in that case would only be turned against him by a British government determined to spin it to their advantage. The fact that Hitler had called for preliminary plans to be drawn up by the German high command for an invasion of England on July 16 is a strong indication of his doubts that his offer would be well received. It seems that he expected to be rejected once again. The preamble to Hitler's War Directive No. 16, which set in motion serious planning for "Operation Sea Lion" [the invasion of England], reads as follows:

> Since England, in spite of her apparently hopeless military situation, shows no sign of coming to terms, I have decided to prepare a landing operation against England, and if necessary carry it out.
>
> The aim of this operation is to eliminate the British homeland as a base for the further prosecution of the war against Germany, and, if necessary to occupy it completely.[334]

Hitler's introductory words demonstrate a lurking lack of confidence existed in his mind *prior* to the day of his address.

Likewise, the Führer's personal letter to Mussolini, dated July 13, seems to demonstrate Hitler's doubts:

> I have made to Britain so many offers of agreement, even of cooperation, and have been treated so shabbily that I am now convinced that any new appeal to reason would meet with a similar rejection.[335]

Halder's diary of the same day records that Hitler was "obsessed with the question of why England does not yet want to take the road to peace." Halder goes on to describe what impressions Hitler had left on the group during a meeting attended by all of Germany's most distinguished generals:

> He [Hitler] sees, just as we do, the solution of this question in the fact that England is still setting her hope in Russia. Thus, he too expects that England will have to be compelled by force to make peace. He does not like to do such a thing, however. Reason: If we smash

England militarily, the British Empire will disintegrate. Germany, however, would not profit from this.[336]

Hitler's Proposal Held at Arm's Length

One again the British people and government balked at the vision of the future which Hitler's offer of peace implied.

Sefton Belmer of the BBC made an immediate unofficial negative response to Hitler's speech. The major British papers treated Hitler's offer with derision. Instead of "exposing" the "Churchill clique" of "warmongers," the average British citizen seems to have been "unmoved by [Hitler's] protestations of how greatly he desired peace." To the average Brit the German dictator's speech was filled with the "usual stuffing about Britain...having deep-layed schemes to invade the Low Countries etc., etc. All the usual lies."[337]

Directly following the speech, the German Foreign Office put out a message to its missions throughout the world, to get feedback on the British reaction. On the whole, the reports that came to Weizsäcker and Ribbentrop's attention were the same: "the moment seems rather unfavorable for peace proposals, as the morale of the English people is better than ever and this is joined with a firm determination not to accept any compromise."[338]

This feedback came by way of Spain and is representative of the average message that came back regarding Hitler's speech. Sometimes, though, the German sources could not refrain from putting in their two cents. The Dublin source reported that the "English attitude would be influenced considerably by a reasonable attitude on the part of Roosevelt."[339]

Was it possible that if Roosevelt would have offered to be the arbiter of peace, the British could have been brought around?

As Hitler was making his address in Berlin, Hans Thomsen, the German chargé d'affaires in Washington, notified the British ambassador to the US, Lord Lothian, that he could provide the specifics of Germany's terms. If the British government wanted the specifics, Thomsen would forward them by way of Lothian. Thomsen had also been tasked by the German Foreign Ministry to get in touch with the Roosevelt administration and inquire whether FDR would consider serving as a mediator.

Lothian called the British Foreign Office with Hitler's terms. The original hard copy of this cross-Atlantic telephone conversation remains elusive, but a memorandum written by Lord Halifax has survived the war. This memo refers to the forwarding of specifics. Whether or not the terms were ever officially received and reviewed is indeterminate for lack of documentary evidence. Some indication that they had been received and reviewed can be found in one source—Nicholson's diaries of July 22, 1940. The Halifax memo put it this way:

> Lothian claims that he knows the German peace terms and that they are most satisfactory.

When Churchill got wind of Lothian's call, he immediately telegrammed the British Foreign Office with this terse reprimand:

> Lord Lothian should be told on no account to make any reply to the German chargé d'affaires' message.

The terms sent by Thomsen to the attention of US Secretary of State Cordell Hull seem to be lost in the mists of time. It is likely that Roosevelt's response would have been identical to Churchill's.

In fact, Roosevelt had given a speech of his own in Chicago on July 19. This was a speech to accept the nomination for an unprecedented third run for the presidency. FDR spoke of his unflagging support of the British. These were more than just words; he backed them up with real support within four days of the speech. On July 23, the British Purchasing Mission to the US reached an agreement with his administration, allowing the Churchill government to purchase forty percent of the US production of military aircraft, and Roosevelt signed into law the "Two Ocean Navy Expansion Act." These were clear signs that FDR intended to help Churchill *resist* coming to any premature peace.

What Churchill was pulling off at the time is incredible in hindsight. He was able to pull Roosevelt and Stalin closer at just the right time in order to avoid having to consider coming to terms with Hitler.

The Soviets were the closest they had ever been since the fateful days of August 1939 to once again switching sides, due to their anxiety over the implications of an Anglo-German peace. German intelligence was picking up on this development. Ribbentrop's office had been informed that Sir Stafford Cripps "had found Stalin inclined to collaborate with England."[340] This and other leads led most high-ranking Germans to conclude that Britain was holding out because she was having diplomatic success in Washington and Moscow. Still, the British government had maintained an official silence for three days—a silence that was in many ways more profoundly disturbing than an immediate rejection of Hitler's offer. Joseph Goebbels' ministry was baffled as to how "to get at the British mentality." Frustration was mounting over the fact that "the British [were] unable to believe that the offer made in the Führer's speech was not just bluff but was meant seriously."[341] What

Goebbels did not understand was that the British government *did* know Hitler wanted to end the war—they just were not about to let him off the hook. They did not think Hitler was bluffing at all.

Hitler's Offer Officially Rejected

The official silence was broken by Viscount Halifax in a radio address to the British people on July 22, 1940. Lord Halifax made the speech instead of Churchill because he was universally considered Churchill's successor. In this way, the Churchill government was serving notice to the world that *his* removal would not necessarily affect a British climb-down. Moreover, in his address, Halifax reiterated the British concept of "justice" based on "security." It was the same line used from the very start! This was a demonstration of the consistency and continuity of thought among the British leadership from the Munich crisis to the summer of 1940. Halifax's words speak for themselves:

> Many of you will have read two days ago the speech in which Hitler…says he has no desire to destroy the British Empire, but there was…no suggestion that peace based on justice, no word of recognition that other nations of Europe had any right to self-determination, the principle he has so often invoked for Germans.[342]

Halifax's words were representative of what had been the British government's ideological prerequisites for peace all along. The notions present in Halifax's radio message are essential in understanding what had been the Allied mood of intransigence during the period of the Phony War. The Halifax address was a definite rejection of Hitler's call for peace.

The Halifax response set in motion the "working out of a democratic plan for countering a peace movement which was certain to come." Hitler's offer to end the war generated a new plan in London, entitled, "Propaganda Future Policy." The British government set down on paper a *script* for dealing with all future German peace offensives. This scripted response policy entailed, among other things, the establishment of a "Brains Trust" to counter future German calls for peace. This new, unofficial department was created on July 26, 1940.

This idea was not new. The suggestion had been recommended by Churchill, Duff Cooper, and Vansitart, after Hitler's first peace speech of October 6, 1939.[343] Even this policy demonstrates that Churchill and others completely understood that Hitler was not bluffing in his call for peace. Halifax's speech demonstrates that the statesman who had been Churchill's most important skeptic was now on the same page. Either that, or he was now *entirely* under Churchill's thumb.

Cadogan notes in his diary on July 26 that "I should judge Hitler doesn't like the looks of invasion and is trying to tempt us to parley."[344] He got this assessment directly from Churchill, and Churchill was correct.

Back at the German Foreign Office, Weizsäcker was puzzled by Halifax's "negative answer," which "seemed to amount to a disavowal of Lothian's feeler."[345] The German State Secretary's remark applies to the connection to London that the German Foreign Office and Foreign Ministry thought they had established by way of Hans Thomsen in Washington. The German government had sent its terms to Lothian upon his request, and Lothian had recognized that the terms were extremely easy. Nevertheless, this is the same connection that had been shut down by Churchill when he got wind of it.

At the end of July 1940, the German position on carrying out a risky invasion of Britain had not at all solidified. Of this, the British War Cabinet was well aware of Hitler's dilemma and did not shrink from using his indecisiveness against him to gain time and avoid a negotiated settlement. The continuing intransigence and reaffirmation of the principles involved in the maintenance of Britain's "will to war" sent Hitler's government back to the drawing board.

Back to the Drawing Board

Since the British still seemed to view any offer of peace as "pure bluff," peace would have to be *forced* upon them. First, there would have to be a realistic *threat* of invasion, Hitler thought. Ribbentrop agreed, saying at the time that "air raids would give English opinion, which was still uncertain, the necessary push in the right direction."[346] The German Propaganda Ministry even set up "secret transmitters" which broadcast "attacks on National Socialism" while attempting to conjure up images of an imminent German invasion. These broadcasts went out with complete and precisely detailed air raid precautions designed to gain the trust of the British population! Incredibly, this tactic obviously worked at counter purposes with the *military effectiveness* of these raids.[347] Goebbels' position reflected Ribbentrop's: "Britain will not see reason until she has suffered the first blows."[348]

Little did the Nazi blunderers know that the British *and* American governments were already confident that the German invasion of England was just a smoke and mirrors game.[349] Both Churchill and Roosevelt, through dependable intelligence sources inside Hitler's own regime, had learned in early August that Hitler did not have confidence in the invasion plan. They were equally informed of Hitler's intimations to his general staff of turning his army against the USSR instead. They knew what most leading military advisors to Hitler knew, the invasion was *not feasible*—at least not yet.

The German naval chief, Raeder, counseled against the idea, arguing that the German navy could not even guarantee the safety of the narrow corridor for crossing the English Channel. The German naval, air force, and army planners clashed endlessly over the plan. In the end it was determined that invasion was impossible until the German Luftwaffe had secured air superiority over the whole of southern England. When air superiority was never achieved, Hitler decided to postpone the invasion until further notice. On October 12, 1940, the head of the German army issued the following order:

> The Führer has decided that until next spring the preparations for Sea Lion are to be continued with the sole intention of maintaining political and military pressure on Britain.[350]

Field Marshal Erich Manstein, in his war memoir entitled *Lost Victories*, attempts to explain Hitler's reluctance to really put all of his energies behind an invasion of England:

> The point is that he did not want to land in Britain. His political concept was at odds with the strategic requirements that followed from the victory in the west. The disastrous part of it was that this concept of his encountered no sympathy in Britain.[351]

What really stood in the way of an end to the war in the summer of 1940 was the British government's refusal to accept a Nazi vision of the future. Hitler's offer was not accepted, because his vision of the future of Europe was unacceptable. They knew it was a long-established vision, and they knew it was *not* going to change just because of a temporary peace settlement.

Alfred Rosenberg, the Nazi Party philosopher, wrote of this vision in his infamous work, *Myth of the Twentieth Century*:

> No Central Europe without distinction of race and nation, as one Naumann has proclaimed, no Franco-Jewish Pan-Europe, but a Nordic Europe is the watchword for the future, with a German Central Europe. Germany or a racial and National State as the central power of the mainland, Italy as security for the south and the southeast; the Scandinavian States with Finland as a second alliance for the security of the northeast, and Great Britain for the security of the west and

overseas at points where it is necessary in the interest of the Nordic peoples.[352]

Britain would not make peace, because she did not want to partake in this vision!

INDEX

Notes

[1] The German navy chief's remarks of September 3, 1939— Martienssen's. *Hitler and His Admirals* (p.19-21)

[2] Franz Halder. Quote from Halder's War Diary in *Young's Illustrated World War II Encyclopedia*. Westport, 1978. Vol. I. (p.41)

[3] Khrushchev. Quote from Schecter and Luchkov's *Khrushchev Remembers*. Boston, 1990 (p. 50)

[4] *Nazi Conspiracy and Aggression*. Vol. VI. Testimony of Walter Funk, German Economics Minister, taken at Nuremberg, Oct. 22, 1945 by Lt. Col. Murray Gurfein. (pp. 219-220).

[5] Robert Rhodes James, ed. *CHIPS: The Diaries of Sir Henry Channon*. Weidenfeld and Nicholson: London, 1967 p. 209
—British War Cabinet Minutes: 17 September, 1939, 18(39)8; CAB 65/1.
—Finland's Ambassador Snow's communiqué to Halifax: 6 November, 1939, in FO 371/23693/6667, PRO (Public Records Office).

[6] *Dokumente zur Deutschlandpolitik* I. Reihe/Band I. (3 September 1939 bis 31 Dezember 1949) Alfred Metzer Verlag: Frankfurt-am-Main; FO 800/325's.

[7] Adolf Hitler, *Mein Kampf*. Trans. Ralph Manheim. Houghton-Mifflin: Boston, 1971. pp.618-625.

[8] Ibid. pp 140-141.

[9] Adolf Hitler, *Mein Kampf*. Trans. Ralph Manheim. Houghton-Mifflin: Boston, 1971. pp.663,665.

[10] Henry Ashby Turner Jr., *Hitler: Memoirs of a Confidant*. Translation by Ruth Heim. Yale U. Press: New Haven, 1979. pp.51-53.

[11] *DeWitte Poole Special Interrogation of Konstantin von Neurath*. National Archives, microfilm M–679 (10-18-4), Roll 2.

[12] *DeWitte Poole Special Interrogation of Konstantin von Neurath*. National Archives, microfilm M–679 (10-18-4), Roll 2.

[13] Paul Schmidt, *Hitler's Interpreter*. Edited by R.H.C. Steed, MacMillan: New York, 1951. p.158.

[14] Max Gallo, *Mussolini's Italy*. MacMillan: New York, 1973. p. 301. Gallo recounts that "Ribbentrop turned aside every argument by the Italians with a general statement: the war against Poland would not spread...." Gallo also cites a prewar meeting (August 12 & 13, 1939) attended by Hitler, Ciano (the Italian foreign minister), Martin Bormann, and Eugen Dollmann, in which Hitler had said, "It [the war against Poland] will be a localized war."

[15] Albert Speer, *Inside the Third Reich*, p. 164-165.

[16] Hugh R. Trevor-Roper, *Blitzkrieg to Defeat: Hitler's War Directives 1939–45*. Hold, Rhinehart and Winston: New York, 1964. The document as reprinted in Trevor-Roper's book makes shows Hitler's desire to leave the opening of any hostilities in the west up to the British and French. Hitler restricts the freedom of action of the German navy, army and air force. Only defensive action was permitted.

[17] David Irving, *The War Path: Hitler's Germany 1933–1939*. The Viking Press: New York, 1978. p. 265.

[18] Erich Raeder, *My Life*. Translated by Henry W. Drexel, Banta Books: Annapolis, 1960 p. 283.

[19] Erich Raeder, *My Life*. Translated by Henry W. Drexel, Banta Books: Annapolis, 1960 p. 284.

[20] Friedrich Ruge (Vice Admiral Friedrich Ruge), *The German Navy's Story: 1939–1945*. Trans. Commander M.G. Sounders. US Naval Institute: Annapolis, 1963. pp. 60-61.

[21] Hansard Diary of October 3, 1939.

[22] Translation from the French: "If you don't attack, we won't either!"

[23] Franz von Papen, *Memoirs*. Translated by Brian Connell. E.P. Dutton: New York, 1953. p. 456.

[24] From the text of Coulondre's message to George Bonnett, the French Minister for Foreign Affairs, received by telephone at 7:45 PM on September 1, 1939.

[25] Field-Marshall Wilhelm Keitel, *Memoirs*. Translated by David Irving. Stein and Day: New York, 1966 p.15

[26] Ernst von Weizsäcker, *Memoirs*. Trans. John Andrews. Henry Regnery Company: New York, 1951, p. 214

[27] *Trials of the Major War Criminals* at Nuremberg. Vol. 15, p.350.

[28] Field-Marshall Wilhelm Keitel, *Memoirs*. Translated by David Irving. Stein and Day: New York, 1966 p.18

[29] Albert Speer, *Inside the Third Reich*, (p.165).

[30] FDRL: *Berle Diary*, Box 211. Memo of September 4, 1939.

[31] Edouard Daladier was the premier of France.

[32] Cordell Hull, *Memoirs*. Vol. I MacMillan: New York, 1948. p. 701

[33] *Documents of German Foreign Policy 1918–1945*. Series D., Vol. 8 (Sept. 4, 1939–March 18, 1940) US Dept. of State Publication No. 5436, US Gov. Printing Office, Washington, DC, 1954. Doc. No. 38, p.24

[34] A.J.P. Taylor, *The Origins of the Second World War*. p. 199

[35] *Documents of German Foreign Policy 1918-1945*. Series D., Vol. 8 (Sept. 4, 1939–March 18, 1940) US Dept. of State Publication No. 5436, US Gov. Printing Office, Washington, DC, 1954. Doc. No. 73.

[36] J.L. Schechter and V.V. Luchkov. *Khrushchev Remembers*. Little, Brown & Co.: Boston, 1990 (p. 48) The famous future premier of the Soviet Union was there and in command of a significant portion of the Soviet forces and bears witness to the fact that they were militarily ready to go, despite the fact that the Soviet government consistently told the German government that they had to delay their part in the dismemberment of Poland because they were not ready.

[37] *Documents on Polish-Soviet Relations*, Vol. I, 1939–1943. Doc. No. 37, (p.42). Telegram of September 3, 1939, from Ribbentrop to the German ambassador to the USSR, Schulenberg, in Moscow, urging Soviets to invade eastern Poland.

Doc. No. 41 (p. 44) of September 15, 1939, contains the propaganda suggestion.

—This same document can also be found in the *Official Documents Concerning Polish-German and Polish-Soviet Relations, 1935–1939* (a.k.a. The Polish White Book) London, 1940. Doc. No. 38 (p. 43)

[38] Ribbentrop's veiled threat can be found in *DGFP*, Vol. 8 Doc. No. 70.

[39] A real gem can be found on this subject in the diary of US Secretary of State Berle, dated September 4, 1939. Berle was smart enough to pick up on why the Soviets were timing their diplomacy so carefully. He writes: "During Saturday the news came of the Russian military mission arriving in Berlin, along with some hysterical French forecasts that the Russians would at once come into the war on the side of the Germans. In which case Bullitt [US

ambassador to France], who is very much excited, thought the defeatist party in the French government would decide there ought to be no war." Berle goes on to note that the Soviet "military mission arrived and was received with all enthusiasm by the Germans; but the Russians did not arrange to come in during the day. The ultimata were to expire very early Sunday morning." From *FDRL*, Berle Diary (September 1939–May 1940) Box 211, memo of September 4, 1939, p.2

[40] An extract from Soviet Foreign Minister Molotov's speech before the Supreme Council of the USSR is indicative of the second part of Stalin's strategy to avoid a declaration of war by the Allies: "...our troops entered the territory of Poland only after the Polish State had collapsed and had in fact ceased to exist." From: *Documents on Polish-Soviet Relations*, Vol. I. No. 66 (pp. 65-69) and

—Jane Degras ed., *Soviet Documents on Foreign Policy*. Vol. III, New York, 1978 (p.388-391)

[41] *DGFP*, Vol. 8 Nos. 104 & 131 of September 20 & 25, 1939. This telegram from the German ambassador to the USSR, Schulenberg, to Ribbentrop expresses Stalin's disapproval of the notion of creating a residual Poland.

[42] Pavel Sudoplatov and Antoli Sudoplatov, *Special Tasks: The Memoirs of an Unwanted Witness—A Soviet Spymaster.* (p. 95)

[43] Pavel Sudoplatov and Antoli Sudoplatov, *Special Tasks: The Memoirs of an Unwanted Witness—A Soviet Spymaster.* (p. 96-97)

[44] Ibid. p. 95, 97.

[45] There are many publications where the text of Hitler's Danzig speech can be located. Here is an on-line source: www.humanitas-international.org/showcase/chronography/speeches/1939-09-19.html

[46] William L. Shirer, *The Rise and the Fall of the Third Reich*. Simon and Schuster: New York, 1961 (pp. 638-639)

[47] Winston S. Churchill, *The Gathering Storm*. Houghton-Mifflin: Boston, 1948. (p. 484)

[48] It is likely that the divisions were so deep and heated that a unified version of an Allied "Vision of the Future" for Europe *never* developed sufficiently. A confirmation of this division is found in the perceptions of an outside observer who was privy to the details of the arguments going on among the British and French leadership. US Secretary of State Berle's diary reads as follows: "I have been endeavoring to review the situation with the possibility

of making some peace for a change. The French aims are now tolerably plain, though not stated. They propose to have a monarchy, with Otto of Hapsburg as Emperor of Austria and Czechoslovakia; and possibly even Poland. I gather that Hungary is to be left out of this, on the General theory that it rests in an Italian sphere of influence. The British are not so definite, and what they want on the continent they have not said." What is perhaps remarkable about Berle's entry is that it was written on November 15, 1939—three and one half months into the war. *FDRL* Berle Diary, Box 211(B) Internal Memo.

[49] Robert Rhodes James ed. *CHIPS: The Diaries of Sir Henry Channon*. Weidenfeld and Nicholson: London, 1967 (p. 222)

[50] Mussolini's speech to the Fascist hierarchy of Bologna established that the Italian government was "ready to assist in peace negotiations."—See "Italy's Role in the European Conflict" by R.G. Woolbert, in *Foreign Policy Reports*. Vol. XVI No. 4 of May 1, 1940.

[51] Robert Rhodes James ed. *CHIPS: The Diaries of Sir Henry Channon*. Weidenfeld and Nicholson: London, 1967 (p. 222)

[52] Ibid. (p. 222)

[53] *Documents on German Foreign Policy*. (September 26, 1939) Doc. No 138 66/46603-19 (p. 140)

[54] Winston Churchill, *The Gathering Storm* (p. 486)

[55] Alfred Rosenberg, *Das Politische Tagebuch*. Hans-Guenther Seraphim verlag: Goettigen-Berlin-Frankfurt, 1936. Entry of September 29, 1939.

[56] Iain MacLeod, *Neville Chamberlain*. Atheneum: New York, 1962 (p. 278)

[57] *Documents on German Foreign Policy*. Vol. 8: Telegrams of October 1, 1939: 463/225787 & 225788; and October 3, 1939: 463/225827 (pp. 268-269)

[58] Franz von Papen, Memoirs. New York, 1953 (p. 456)

[59] *DeWitte Pool Special Interrogation of von Papen*. US National Archives, Microfilm M-679 (10-18-4), Roll 3. Corroboration can be found in *Documents on German Foreign Policy*. Vol. 8 : Telegrams of October 1, 1939: 463/225787 & 225788; and October 3, 1939: 463/225827 (pp. 268-269)

[60] Joseph E. Perisco, *Roosevelt's Secret War: FDR and World War II Espionage*. Random House, New York, 2002 (p. 45)

[61] *FDRL* Small Collections File: William Rhodes Davis. A German record of what Davis said to Göring was taken by ministerial

director Wohlstat (Notes of October 1, 1939, of the conference with Davis). After the war these notes were found among the captured German documents and transferred to microfilm. The notes were originally stored in the US National Archives and later were passed on to the FDRL in 1966.

[62] *FDRL*: Small Collections File on William Rhodes Davis. This is from Davis' report on his Peace Mission to Roosevelt, written on October 11, 1939. Attached to pages 11 and 12 of this report are telegrams sent by Davis to Roosevelt on October 2, 3, and 4, 1939.

[63] The details of Davis' account of the meeting are corroborated in Alfred Rosenberg's Diary entries of October 5, 1939—see Alfred Rosenberg, *Letzte Aufzeichnungen*. Gottingen: Plesse Verlag, 1951 (p. 83)

[64] *FDRL*: Small Collections File on William Rhodes Davis. This is from Davis' report on his peace mission to Roosevelt, written on October 11, 1939. Attached to pages 11 and 12 of this report are telegrams sent by Davis to Roosevelt on October 2, 3, and 4, 1939.

[65] Ibid. Davis' summary of his mission in a letter to Roosevelt—written on Oct. 11 and stamped "received" on October 12, 1939.

[66] For the text of the secret protocol attached to the treaty see—*Documents of Polish-Soviet Relations, 1939–1945*, Vol. I, No. 54 (p. 53), No. 59 (pp. 57-60). For the document which confirmed Lithuania's place in the Soviet sphere of influence see—*Documents of Polish-Soviet Relations*, No. 62 (p. 63). The Soviet-Lithuanian Agreement of Moscow was signed on October 10, 1939.

[67] *Documents on German Foreign Policy 1918–1945*. Weizsäcker Memo: 2177/471598-600 (p. 179)

[68] *Dokumente zur Deutschlandpolitik*. Sir S. Cripps' Oct. "Note on Hitler's Offer"; FO 800/325 (p. 21)

[69] Schmidt, *Hitler's Interpreter*. Edited by R.H.C. Steed, MacMillan: New York, 1951. (p. 166)

[70] William L. Shirer, *The Rise and The Fall of the Third Reich*. (p. 640-641)
Raoul de Roussy de Sales. *Hitler: My New Order*. Reynal and Hitchcock: New York, 1941. (p 722-756)

[71] Georges Bonnet, *Dans la Tourmente* (p. 209)

[72] *Izvestia*: Izvestia was a government-owned and controlled publishing house—most known for its publication of an official Soviet newspaper. It was then the USSR's major daily newspaper.

[73] It is unclear why so many people have forgotten some of the more radical things Shaw said and wrote of in the 1930s. By 1933 he was calling Stalin and Mussolini "the most responsible statesmen in Europe," and, if he moderated his enthusiasm for the Duce, his faith in Uncle Joe remained intact.

[74] *DGFP*, Vol. 8, Telegram No. 332, sent October 7, 1939. Doc. No. 210.

[75] *DGFP*, Vol. 8, Telegram No. 332, sent October 7, 1939. Doc. No. 210.

[76] *New York Times,* Article of October 5, 1939 (p. 1)

[77] Fred Taylor (editor and translator) *The Goebbels Diaries*. G.P. Putnam: New York, 1983. October 14 & 15 diary entries, pp. 19-20.

[78] David Dilks (ed) *The Diaries of Sir Alexander Cadogan 1938–1945*. Putnam: New York, 1972. October 7, 1939 diary entry, p. 221.

[79] Lamb, *The Ghosts of Peace* (p. 127)

[80] *FDRL*: Berle Papers, Box 211. Memo to FDR, dated Oct. 6, 1939 (pp.7-8)

[81] Georges Bonnet, *Quai d'Orsay*. Times Press: New York, 1965 (p. 279)

[82] Joseph Lash, *Churchill and Roosevelt 1939–1941*. W.W. Norton & Co.: New York, 1976 (p. 75)

[83] MacLeod, *Neville Chamberlain*. (p. 279)

[84] Winterhilfe was the name of a dual initiative (government and the private sector) public welfare program, designed for the benefit of the poor and hungry. The program first seems to have developed in Switzerland. Its objectives included "supply of needy in Essküchen" (mobile hot food kitchens), "encouraging the poor to switch to cheaper fuel material" and "delivery of articles of clothing" to the destitute—almost exclusively in the inner-city.

[85] *New York Times*, Headline article on October 6, 1939. (p.1)

[86] Cordell Hull, *The Memoirs of Cordell Hull*. Vol. I (p. 711)—Langer and Gleason, *The Challenge of Isolation 1937–1940*. (p. 255)

[87] *New York Times*, October 7, 1939 (p. 1)

[88] *Documents on German Foreign Policy*. Vol. 8 (pp. 197-198)

[89] MacLeod, *Neville Chamberlain* (p. 279)

[90] *Department of State Foreign Relations of the US Diplomatic Papers: 1940*. Chamberlain letter to Lord Lothian, dated Feb. 4, 1940. Vol. 5, Dept. of State Pub., US Government Printing Office,

Washington, DC, 1959–61.

[91] "Sir Stafford Cripps as British Ambassador to Moscow, May 1940–June 1941" by H. Hanak, *The English Historical Review*, Vol. XCIV, 1979 (pp. 43-70), (p. 53).

[92] *Documents on German Foreign Policy*, Doc. No. 242), (p. 268)

[93] *Documents on German Foreign Policy*, Doc. No. 255, (p. 286)

[94] *Documents on German Foreign Policy*, Doc. No. 259, (p. 289)

[95] Ibid., Doc. 259, (p. 289)

[96] William L. Shirer, *Berlin Diary: The Journal of a Foreign Correspondent, 1939–1941.* A.A. Knopf: New York, 1941. October 11, 1939 entry (p. 236)

[97] *FDRL*: Adolf Berle Papers, Box 211, Diary entry of Oct 10, 1939 (p.3)

[98] William Russel, *Berlin Embassy*. E.P. Dutton & Co.: New York, 1941 (pp. 92-97)

[99] Goebbels *Diary* (p. 18)

[100] Joseph Goebbels, *Diary*. Entries of October 15 & 16, 1939 (p. 20-21)—see pages in *Peace at Daggers Drawn* that go along with footnotes 16-19 to get a broader understanding of Goebbels vitriolic words against the German navy.

[101] Albert Speer reports in his postwar memoir, *Inside the Third Reich* (p. 162), that Joseph Goebbels was openly "acrid" toward Ribbentrop and regarded him as the leader of the "war party" in Germany at the time.

[102] *DeWitte Pool Special Interrogation of von Dirksen*, M-679 (10-18-5), Roll 1 (p. 17)—Herbert von Dirksen had replaced Ribbentrop as the ambassador to Great Britain in 1938–39.

[103] Weizsacker, *Memoirs* (p. 217)

[104] Von Papen, *Memoirs*. (p. 458)

[105] In Joachim von Ribbentrop's letter to his wife Annelies, of October 5, 1939, he tried to explain why the war that he had told everyone would not come, had come: "Many of the events were bound to happen; when Hitler recognized that his original idea, the creation of a powerful Reich of all Germans allied to Britain, could not be realized, he tried to build and secure this Reich with his own military resources. In this way he created for himself a world of enemies. I, too, wanted a strong Germany, but I hoped to achieve it gradually, by diplomatic means." —Joachim von Ribbentrop. *Ribbentrop Memoirs*. London, 1954 (p. 141)

[106] Joseph Goebbels, *Diaries*. (p. 30-31)

[107] Starzinski committed suicide the day after the surrender according to a page 1 report in the *New York Times* (October 5, 1939).

[108] The full text of the Anglo-Polish Mutual Assistance Treaty, signed in Warsaw on August 25, 1939, can be found online at the *Avalon Project at Yale Law School's* website—at http://www.yale.edu/lawweb/avalon/wwii/bluebook/blbk19.htm

[109] In an amazing twist, the Romanian government had a treaty of mutual assistance of its own with Poland. The Romanian government, as previously mentioned, cooperated with British authorities (on the ground in Romania) to facilitate the escape of the Polish government. The Polish-Romanian treaty guaranteed military assistance to Poland in case of a *Soviet attack*. Since the Soviets did attack Poland, how then did Romania avoid declaring war on the USSR? Ironically, the Romanians avoided declaring against the USSR by claiming that the Polish government with whom they had signed the agreement in question *no longer existed*! Who says "you can't have it both ways?"

[110] *Documents on Polish-Soviet Relations.* Vol. I, Doc. No. 57 of Sept. 30, 1939 (p.55)

[111] Hans Roost, *A Modern History of Poland.* Trans. J.R. Foster, Alfred A. Knopf: New York, 1966 (p. 171).

[112] Ulrich von Hassel. *The von Hassel Diaries 1938–1945.* Doubleday: New York, 1947 (p.80-81)—Ulrich von Hassel was a career diplomat. He served in Spain, Denmark, Yugoslavia, and finally as German ambassador to Italy from 1932 to 1938. Von Hassel was dismissed for opposing the Rome-Berlin Axis. As ambassador to Italy von Hassel had predicted that Hitler's foreign policy would lead Germany to war. During World War II, Hassel used his international experience to make clandestine contact with British and American officials. Von Hassel played a major role in the planning of a coup against Hitler, hoping that it would translate into an honorable peace treaty with the western Allies.

[113] F. Taylor, ed. *The Goebbels Diaries.* (p. 30-31)

[114] Georg Achate Gripenberg. *Memoirs of the Finnish Ambassador* (p. 72)

[115] Richard Lamb. *The Ghosts of Peace.* Michael Russel: Guildford, 1987 (p. 131) Citing *PREM* I/443.

[116] *FDRL*: Adolf Berle File 211(B), memo of Dec. 26, 1939 (p. 3)

[117] *FDRL*: Adolf Berle Diary 211(C), March 12, 1940 entry.

[118] Ivan Maisky. *Memoirs of a Soviet Ambassador 1939–1943* (p. 13), *Khrushchev Remembers* (p. 46-49), *Tribune.* March 24, 1939 "Interview with Sir Stafford Cripps."

[119] Insightful analysis of Stalin's thought process can be found in Pavel Sudoplatov and Antoli Sudoplatov, *Special Tasks: The Memoirs of an Unwanted Witness—A Soviet Spymaster.* (p. 96-97)

[120] Italy was bound by treaty with Germany to immediately enter the war. This was stipulated in Article III of the famous Pact of Steel. The Italian Secretary of State later admitted in a public speech (Dec. 16, 1939) to an additional secret clause to the treaty in which the Italian government promised to come to Germany's aid if Germany was attacked by a third party.

[121] *DeWitte Pool Special Interrogation of Dr. Paul Schmidt.* US National Archives. M-679, Roll 3, p.32. This is presented in Schmidt's book *Hitler's Interpreter* as well on page 168.

[122] The following sources were used in the entire section on the planned coup:
Peter Hoffman. "Peace Through Coup d'État: The Foreign Contacts of the German Resistance, 1933–44." *Central European History* 19 (March 1986): pp. 3-44.
Peter Hoffman. *The History of the German Resistance, 1933–45.* Trans. from German. Cambridge, 1977.
Peter Hoffman. *German Resistance.*
Annedore Leber ed. *The Conscience in Revolt: Portraits of the German Resistance, 1933–1945.* Munich, Germany: Von Hase & Koehler, 1994.
Joachim Fest. *Plotting Hitler's Death.* Metropolitan Books: New York, 1996

[123] *The Goebbels Diaries 1939–1941.* Nov. 9 entry.
Weizsäcker *Memoirs* (p. 219)

[124] *Goebbels Diaries 1939–1941.* Nov. 9 entry.

[125] *Goebbels Diaries 1939–1941.* Nov. 9 entry.

[126] This is a reference to the accusation that the Nazis had burned down their own parliament building as an excuse to crack down on political adversaries, suspend certain constitutional rights, and to institute new and far-reaching government powers for Hitler.

[127] MacLeod. *Neville Chamberlain* (p. 281)

[128] *Newsweek* magazine article from the January 22, 1940 issue: page 23.

[129] Using January of 1939 as a base, the value of German imports decreased by 61% as of January 1940. Exports fell by 29% Fuel

supplies fell by 33%; by January 1940, Germany was receiving 10,000 tons of refined petroleum from Romania, whereas during the same month 255,000 tons and 160,000 tons went to Britain and France respectively. Other sources indicate that by January 1940, Germany was cut off from half of its normal peacetime imports. See John C. Wilde's "Germany's Wartime Economy" in *Foreign Policy Reports*, Vol. XVI, no. 7 of January 15, 1940; or Randle Elliot's "The Oslo States and the European War" in *Foreign Policy Reports*, Vol. XV, no. 21 of Jan. 15, 1940; or US *National Archives* T-84, 'zahlen zur Entwicklung des deutschen Aussenhandels seit kriegsbeginn"; or US *National Archives* T-77, Roll 438, "Mineralöl und die Versorgungslage im krieg."; *FDRL*: PRO microfilm 66/6 W.P. (40)40, March 28, 1940 British government report on "German Oil Supplies"—an attached graphic show Germany's supply down by more than 50% while over the same period Britain has *five times more in supply than before.*

[130] *New York Times*, September 17, 1939 (p. 34)

[131] "The Race for Northern Europe" by Martii Haiko, in Hendrik *Nissen's Scandinavia During World War II*, U. of Minnesota Press: Minneapolis, 1987; *Vart Folks Historie* Vol. 9 (p. 122) Oslo, 1961–1964. Both of these works shed light on the US cooperation with the Allies in attempts to achieve economic arrangements that would shut Germany out or cause her to take risky military action.

[132] Cordell Hull. *Memoirs*. Vol. I (pp. 590-591)

[133] *Peace and War: US Foreign Policy 1931–1941*. US Gov't Printing Office: Washington, DC, 1943 (pp. 425-426)

[134] Langer and Gleason's *The Challenge of Isolationism* (p.88)

[135] As early as September 20, 1939, a British commercial mission had arrived in Rome hoping to sow the seeds of state I in Chamberlain's Peace Front policy. The British blockade had already cut off around 6 million tons of desperately needed coal. The British delegation proposed to send 12 million tons of Welsh coal if the Italian government so desired. In return, Italy would be expected to deliver an equal value of machinery. A mission was sent to Turkey at the same time and with similar intent.—*New York Times* article of September 20, 1939.

[136] *Relazioni Internazionali*, December 23, 1939 (pp. 1065-1070); the text of the speech appeared in German newspaper too, such as the *Volkerbund*, on December 20, 1939.—Immediately following the speech, Ciano reports in his diary that "the British ambassador congratulated [him] on the speech."—Galaezzo Ciano. *Ciano's*

Diary. Methuen: London, 1952 (December 16, 1939 entry)

[137] The official notice of the USSR's expulsion came on December 14, 1939.

[138] Jane Degras ed. *Soviet Documents on Foreign Policy*. Vol. III, Octagon Books: New York, 1978. (pp.388-389)

[139] Jane Degras ed. *Soviet Documents on Foreign Policy*. Vol. III, Octagon Books: New York, 1978. (pp.409)

[140] *Foreign Relations of the US* 1940. Vol. I (p. 270) Message of the American minister in Sweden, Sterling, to US Secretary of State Cordell Hull, January 22, 1940.

[141] What would have happened if the Allies had sent troops to Finland to fight the Soviets and the German government had decided to send troops as well?

[142] Why? Because the Allied Supreme War Council wanted to use the Finns as a pretext to seize key Norwegian fjord-ports and the iron ore producing regions in both Norway and Sweden. In fact, Churchill and Paul Reynaud wanted to go ahead with the occupation of Norway and Sweden even without this pretext. Thus, Allied strategy was internally divided. One group wanted the Russo-Finnish War to continue and another wanted it to end.—see the *Ironsides Diaries* (pp.224,228,231) and compare *FDRL* CAB 66/6 PRO War Cabinet File: Scandinavia, February 24 SWP (40)71 to WP (40)112 and (40)115 of March 27, 1940. More connections to this split can be found in *FDRL* CAB 66/6 PRO War Cabinet File: "The Military Implications of Hostilities with Russia in 1940," a report generated by the Allied Chiefs of Staff Committee on March 5, 1940.

[143] Daladier was ousted in March 1940, Reynaud became France's new Prime Minister.

[144] *Foreign Relations of the US 1940*. Vol. I, (p. 275)
Paul Reynaud. *In the Thick of the Fight*. Simon & Schuster: New York, 1965 (p. 257)

[145] Paul Reynaud. *In the Thick of the Fight*. Simon & Schuster: New York, 1965 (p. 264)

[146] Georges Bonnett. *Quai d'Orsay*. Times Press: New York, 1965 (p. 285)

[147] R. MacCleod and D. Kelly eds. *The Ironsides Diaries, 1937-40*. London, 1963 (pp. 224-231) Diary entries of March 2, 4, 14, 19, 27, 31, 1940.

[148] Cadogan *Diaries* (p. 239)

[149] Lash's *Roosevelt and Churchill 1939-1941*. (p. 83) Lash found this quote in the official records of the British War Cabinet.

[150] Sumner Welles. *The Time for Decision*. Harper & Bros.: London and New York, 1944 (p. 133)

[151] Cadogan *Diary* entry of December 25, 1939. This entry is confirmed by the minutes of the British War Cabinet from the same day—*CAB* 65/2 War Minutes (39) 120 and (39)150 of Dec. 25, 1939: Cited in Elizabeth Barker. *British Policy in South-East Europe in the Second World War*. Barnes and Noble: New York, 1976, (pp. 20-23).

[152] Cadogan *Diaries*. December 27, 1939 entry.

[153] *Document Diplomati Italiani*. Vol. I no. 608 (pp. 375-376)—The French ambassador in Rome, Francois-Poncet, forwards French Premier Daladier's sentiments to the Italian foreign minister, Ciano, back on September 29, 1939.

[154] The quote comes from the Cadogan *Diaries*. March 8, 1940 entry. Corroboration can be established through Ciano's *Diaries* (March 9, 1940 entry) and *FRUS*, 1940. Vol. I March 13, 1940 (p.88) and an insightful article by R.G. Woolbert, entitled, "Italy's Part in the European Conflict." In *Foreign Policy* Report Vol. XVI no. 4 of May 1, 1940. On page 63 of Woolbert's article he reports that the British had allowed a particularly important convoy of seized Italian coal vessels to continue to Italy on the eve of Ribbentrop's visit to Rome.

[155] *FDRL*: Berle Diary of January–March, 1940. Box 211—Berle's record of his Jan. 22, 1940, official protest to the British government through the British ambassador in Washington, Lord Lothian—It is interesting that according to a US *Department of State Bulletin* which gives an account of the detention of US shipping between September 1, 1939, and May 24, 1940, out of 204 ships stopped and searched only 4 were stopped by German ships, whereas 180 were stopped by British ships—Source: *Docs on American Foreign Relations*. Vol. II, (p.713).

[156] *Newsweek*. January 1, 1940 issue (p. 19)

[157] *Newsweek*. January 1, 1940 issue (p. 13-19)

[158] *Newsweek*. January 1, 1940 issue (p. 13-19)

[159] *The Goebbels Diaries* (January 3 & 4 entries of 1940)

[160] *Documents on German Foreign Policy*. Vol. 8 (p. 604-609); Paul Schmidt. *Hitler's Interpreter* (p. 167)

[161] *Documents on German Foreign Policy*. Vol. 8 (p. 604-609)

[162] Khrushchev's memoirs contain the following insights into the depths of Stalin's dealings: Stalin, August 24, 1939 (the day after the signing of the Nazi-Soviet pact)—"Well, we deceived Hitler for the time being." Khrushchev comments: "As for Stalin's decision to sign the treaty, that was also a political maneuver. He [Stalin] thought he was deceiving Hitler, turning him against the west."—source: Schecter and Luchkov's *Khrushchev Remembers*. Boston, 1990 (p. 50). Soviet Admiral Kuznetsov knew that Stalin regarded the Nazi-Soviet pact as simply a bid to gain time and better strategic position, saying that Stalin fully expected that war with Nazi Germany was an eventuality.—source: Harrison E. Salisbury. *The 900 Days: The Siege of Leningrad.* Harper & Row: New York, 1967 (p. 77)

[163] *FDRL*: Berle Diary, Box 211, December 29, 1939 (p.3)

[164] Cordell Hull. *Memoirs*. Vol. I, (p.591)

[165] *Foreign Relations of the US 1940*, Vol. I (p. 116)

[166] Felix Kersten. *The Kersten Memoirs, 1940–45.* Trans. Constantine Fitzgibbon and James Oliver. MacMillan Co.: New York, 1957. (p. 234-235)

[167] Felix Kersten. *The Kersten Memoirs, 1940–45 (p. 234-235)*

[168] Felix Kersten. *The Kersten Memoirs, 1940–45.* Trans. Constantine Fitzgibbon and James Oliver. MacMillan Co.: New York, 1957. (p. 235-236)

[169] Sumner Welles. *The Time for Decision* (p. 87)

[170] *Foreign Relations of the US 1940*, Vol. II (p. 685). The background information on why Attalico was removed can be found in—"Records of the German Foreign Ministry Received by the US Department of State." US *National Archives*. Microfilm T-120, Roll 909, Frame 380269: Weizsäcker memo of Feb. 12, 1940. This source is corroborated in Weizsäcker's *Memoirs* (p.221)

[171] Sir Llewellyn Woodward ed. *British Foreign Policy in the Second World War*. H.M. Stationary Office: London, 1976 (p. 165)

[172] Sumner Welles. *The Time for Decision*. (p. 74)

[173] [173] Sumner Welles. *The Time for Decision*. (p. 76)

[174] The fact that an offensive plan existed on the Allied side is often a shock to most people, who, for some reason, live under the mistaken impression that the Allies only ever considered a defensive plan for the western front. Part of the reason for this misperception is that the "Dyle Plan," as it was know internally, has *never been addressed in a historical monograph*. When the plan is mentioned in general works on the history of the Second

World War, it is only ever mentioned in passing. The reason for this is simple: most historians are so overwhelmed by the availability of every single document on the German side, that digging into the forbidden zone of Allied war planning is a comparative hardship.

[175] Paul Reynaud. *In the Thick of the Fight* (p. 255)

[176] *Ironsides Diaries*. (p. 211)

[177] *Ironsides Diaries*. (p. 211)

[178] *Ironsides Diaries*. (pp. 216-217)

[179] *Illustrated History of World War II*, Vol. I, (p. 78) Gamelin Memo of March 16, 1940.

[180] *Illustrated History of World War II*, Vol. I, (p. 78)—From Gamelin's notes on the March 18, 1940, after a meeting of the Allied Supreme War Council.

[181] PRO: War Cabinet Minutes of January 3, 1940, WM 48(40)6; WM 2(40)1.

[182] *Cadogan Diary*, entries of January 22, 24, 1940.

[183] *Cadogan Diary* entry of January 30, 1940.

[184] *Cadogan Diary* entry of February 2, 1940.

[185] Cordell Hull *Memoirs*, Vol. I (p. 737) and Sumner Welles' *The Time for Decision* (p. 73)

[186] Woodward's *British Foreign Policy in the Second World War*. (p. 167) and *FRUS* 1940. Vol. I (p. 267-270)—Telegraph from the US chargé d'affaires in London, Johnson, to US Secretary of State Cordell Hull.

[187] Ivan Maisky. *Memoirs of a Soviet Ambassador: The War 1939–43*. New York, 1949 (p. 43)

[188] Paul Reynaud. *In the Thick of the Fight*. (p. 256)

[189] Kermit Roosevelt was in charge of sending British volunteers to Finland—See George Achates Gripenberg. *Memoirs of the Finnish Ambassador* (p.99) or his other memoir, entitled *Finland and the Great Powers: Memoirs of a Diplomat*. (p. 100-109) Gripenberg was the Finnish ambassador to Britain from 1933–1941. According to the *New York Times*, way back on September 21, 1939, Kermit Roosevelt "was reported today to have become a British subject in order to help Britain in the war with Germany." "Mr. Roosevelt, who is a friend of Winston Churchill…is believed to have been offered a post in the Ministry of Shipping."—source: *New York Times*, September 21, 1939 (p.1)

[190] FRUS 1940: vol. I (p. 14-15) Message from Joseph Kennedy, US ambassador to Britain, to Cordell Hull of March 9, 1940.

Confirmation of Roosevelt's developing sense of urgency can be found in French sources as well, in —Paul Reynaud. *In the Thick of the Fight.* (p. 257)

[191] Max Jacobson. *The Diplomacy of the Winter War.* Harvard U. Press: Cambridge, 1961 (p. 190)

[192] Max Jacobson. *The Diplomacy of the Winter War.* Harvard U. Press: Cambridge, 1961 (p. 91); Gripenberg's *Memoirs of the Finnish Ambassador* (p.109)

[193] *FDRL*: Berle Diary, box 211, December 5, 1939 (p. 1)

[194] Luigi Villari. *Italian Foreign Policy Under Mussolini.* The Devin-Adair Co.: New York, 1956. (p.243)

[195] Gabriel Gorodetsky. *Stafford Cripps's Mission to Moscow 1940–42.* Cambridge U. Press: Cambridge, 1984 (p.20)—The British desire for rapprochement with the Soviets is also found in Woodward's *British Foreign Policy in the Second World War* (p.109)

[196] Dewitte Pool Interrogation of Dr. Karl Ritter—Chief of the Economic Section of the German Foreign Office: US *National Archives.* Roll 3, p.3-4 of the "Ritter File."

[197] Sumner Welles. *The Time for Decision* (p. 85)—The attention FDR paid Mussolini in a personal letter which suggested a two-power summit was the only one of its sort. None of the other heads of state on Welles' itinerary received this sort of personal attention by FDR.

[198] Sumner Welles. *The Time for Decision.* (p. 85)

[199] At a White House press conference, FDR had announced, "Mr. Welles will…be authorized to make no proposals or commitments in the name of the US government." After the mission, FDR again repeated this false assertion, saying: "He [Welles] has not offered any proposals…nor has he brought back to me any peace proposals from any source."—See The Dept. of State Bulletins of Feb. 10, 1940 (Vol. II, no. 33/1435 p. 155) and March 30, 1940 (Vol. II, no. 40/1445 p. 335)

[200] Sumner Welles. *The Time for Decision* (p. 88). Welles' version is corroborated in *FRUS* 1940 Vol. I, Message from Welles in Rome of February 26, 1940 (p. 29-31)

[201] Weizsäcker *Memoirs* (p. 223)

[202] *Documents on German Foreign Policy.* Vol. VIII, no. 138 of Dec. 26, 1939 (p. 140) and Paul Schmidt *Hitler's Interpreter* (p. 168)

[203] Erich Kordt. *Wahn und Wirklichkeit.* (p. 239-240)

[204] On the matter of German knowledge of Allied war planning and the decision to preempt them in Scandinavia see—Anthony Martiensen ed. *Führer Conferences on Naval Affairs, 1939*. British Admiralty: London, 1948. Raeder. My Life (p.306); Vital commentary on the timing of the end of the Russo-Finnish War can be found in Alexander Cadogan's *Diary* entry of Feb. 23, 1940, and Paul Reynaud's *In the Thick of the Fight* (p.270); The German government later published the *German White Book No. 5* "Allied Intrigue in the Low Countries." New York German Library of Information, 1940, p. A43-A-48, Doc. No. 20 (p.1-6) detailing the Allied schemes to spread out the war.

[205] *New York Times*, March 1, 1940 (p. 1 & 3)

[206] *New York Times*, March 2, 1940 (p. 3)

[207] Weizsäcker's *Memoirs* (p. 223) are corroborated by Welles' version of the meeting in his *The Time for Decision* (p. 101)

[208] Paul Schmidt. *Hitler's Interpreter* (p. 169)

[209] *FDRL*: PSF/Box 6, March 1, 1940 notes of Welles' meeting with Ribbentrop (p.2)

[210] *FDRL*: PSF/Box 6, March 1, 1940 (p. 7). What was Ribbentrop talking about? Answer: When Warsaw fell in late September of 1939, SS Brigadeführer Freiherr von Keunsberg caught ministers of the Polish Foreign Ministry in the process of destroying documents. The rescued documents were turned over to the German Foreign Office. Hans Adolf von Moltke, the former German ambassador to Poland, headed a special archive commission to examine the documents and translate them. At the end of March 1940, a handful of the most incriminating of these documents were published under the title *Polnische Dokumente zur Vorgeschichte des krieges*. Even an American edition was published and distributed from New York City. Journalists had been given copies of the original Polish documents at a press conference at the German Ministry of Foreign Affairs on March 29, 1940. Excerpts saw wide distribution in the US press. The authenticity of these documents has been verified by the Polish ambassador to London, Edward Raczynski, in his memoir entitled *In Allied London* (p. 51) as well as by the former Polish ambassador to France, Juliusz Lukasiewicz, in his memoir entitled *Diplomat in Paris 1936–1939*, and Polish Foreign Ministry Undersecretary Count Jan Szembeck's *Journal 1933–39* (pp.475-476); FDR really does appear to have played a vital role in encouraging the Polish government to resist negotiating any

revision of her territory with Germany.

[211] *FDRL*: PSF/Box 6, March 1, 1940: Welles' notes on his meeting with Ribbentrop (p. 13)

[212] Sumner Welles. *The Time for Decision* (p. 104)

[213] Note: Did Hitler have any solid reason to believe that the Allied vision of the future peace of Europe was aimed at more than just removing him and Nazism from the equation? The sad answer is an unequivocal "yes." It was widely known in the press that the Allied leadership saw no room for *Germany* in Europe's future, let alone Hitlerism or Nazism. Chamberlain and Daladier had been hinting to the press for some time (since approx. January 1940) at what their vision of a peaceful Europe of the future held. They floated the idea of a "federal scheme for postwar Europe." These schemes included breaking Germany up into four or possibly five separate, autonomous, states. It was not just Chamberlain and Daladier either making public proclamations regarding the breaking up of Germany in order to secure the future peace of Europe. The British Labour Party's slogan was "Europe Must Federate or Perish." They had a "Six-Point Program" detailing their plan for the "atomization" of Germany—i.e. Breaking it up into a loose federation of autonomous states. In the US, *Newsweek* magazine reported on the plan and other similar plans being kicked around by the British leadership at the time, saying that the general principles of a postwar central Europe had already been worked out, even if the details were still open to debate within British and French political circles. One particular article reported that the plan, in one form or another, was supported by a diverse spectrum of characters, including Churchill, Duff Cooper, Anthony Eden, Lord Beaverbrook, and Chamberlain—Source: *Newsweek*, February 12, 1940 (p. 23). In Hitler's conversation with Welles he cited a speech by Sir John Simon, in which the British statesman called for the "total destruction of Germany."

[214] *FDRL*: PSF, Box 6: Welles' notes of his meeting with Hitler. (p. 9)

[215] Cordell Hull. *Memoirs*. Vol. I (p. 740)

[216] Neville Chamberlain wrote to his sister Hilda on March 14, 1940, and told her that he had been assured by way of Welles that Roosevelt agreed that if "Hitler did not disappear he would have to give up most of what Nazidom stands for."—see Richard Lamb's *The Ghosts of Peace*. (p. 135)

[217] Cordell Hull *Memoirs* (p.740)

[218] Sumner Welles. *The Time for Decision.* (p. 104)

[219] Cordell Hull *Memoirs* (p.740)

[220] FDRL: PDF, Box 6. Notes from Welles' meeting with Göring. (p.3); AJP Taylor. *The Origins of the Second World War* (p. 199)

[221] *FDRL*: PSF, Box 6: Welles' notes of his meeting with Hitler. (p. 9)

[222] *FDRL*: PSF, Box 6: Welles' notes of his meeting with Hitler. (p. 6)

[223] *FDRL*: PSF, Box 6: Welles' notes of his meeting with Hitler. (p. 7). The full text of Welles' notes on this conversation can be found online now: see www.fdrlibrary.marist.edu/psf/box6/t72h01.html (a letter detailing Welles' conversation with Göring on March 3, 1940).

[224] *Foreign Relations of the Us, 1940* Vol. I, March 7, 1940 (p. 60-61)

[225] *FDRL*: PSF, Box 6: Welles' notes of his meeting with Daladier. (p. 6). The full text of Welles' notes on this conversation can be found online now: see www.fdrlibrary.marist.edu/psf/box6/t72h01.html .

[226] Note: If Daladier had ever said to Hitler or Ribbentrop what he said here to Welles, can anyone seriously blame the Germans that they came to the conclusion that France would not stand in the way of the reincorporation of Poland's majority-German territories into the German Reich? Daladier's statement was even echoed in a letter sent to Hitler just prior to Germany's attack on Poland. This letter, according to Hitler, made it clear that the French government had no desire to go to war with Germany over the Polish corridor and Danzig—source: Walter Görlitz (ed). *In the Service of the Reich: Originally Published as the Memoirs of Field-Marshal Keitel, Chief of the German High Command, 1938-1945.* Focal Point Publications, 2003 (p. 104)

[227] *FDRL*: PSF, Box 6: Welles' notes of his meeting with Daladier. (p. 8). The full text of Welles' notes on this conversation can be found online now:
see www.fdrlibrary.marist.edu/psf/box6/t72h01.html

[228] *FDRL*: PSF, Box 6: Welles' notes of his meeting with Daladier. (p. 8-9). The full text of Welles' notes on this conversation can be found online now:
see www.fdrlibrary.marist.edu/psf/box6/t72h01.html

[229] Sumner Welles. *The Time for Decision.* (p. 1280)

[230] Parliamentary Debates. British House of Commons. Vol. 345 No. 28, April 3, 1939—col. 2489

[231] Sumner Welles. *The Time for Decision. (p. 131)*

[232] *Foreign Policy of the US 1940*. Vol. I., March 13, 1940. (p. 88)

[233] US *Department of State Bulletin*. Vol. II (p.367)

[234] *FDRL*: PSF/ Box 6. March 11, 1940. Welles' notes of his conversation with Chamberlain. (p. 4)

[235] Welles. *The Time for Decision* (p. 132)

[236] *FDRL/PSF/Box 6* London, March 11, 1940 (p. 1-3)

[237] *FDRL*: PSF/Box 6: Welles' meeting with Churchill of March 12, 1940 (p. 1-2)

[238] *FRUS*, 1940. Vol. I. (p. 87)

[239] *FRUS 1940*. Vol. I (pp. 85-86)

[240] *FDRL*: PSF/ Box 6, Welles' conversations of March 12, 1940 (p. 1)

[241] *FDRL*: PSF/Box 6 Welles' notes of March 14, 1940 (p.1)

[242] *The Channon Diaries*, March 13, 1940 entry; *British and Foreign State Papers* 1940-42. Vol.144 (pp.383-384); *Dokumente zur Deutschlandpolitik*. Doc no. 274 (p.140); *The Ironsides Diaries* (p. 217-218)

[243] *FDRL*: PRO Cab 66) British War Cabinet Memo SWC (39) First Meeting of the Supreme War Council, September 20, 1939.

[244] Even before Welles had returned to Rome, the US Assistant Secretary of State was aware of Ribbentrop's activities in Rome. On March 10, Berle wrote in his diary, "Ribbentrop is going to Rome to talk to the Italians and likewise to the Pope. Everybody connects it with the Scandinavian situation, which I think is probably a misapprehension." Source—*FDRL*: Berle Diary/ Box 211.

[245] Welles. *The Time for Decision*. (p.136); *The Ciano Diaries*. Vol. I (224)

[246] Paul Schmidt. *Hitler's Interpreter* (p. 170)

[247] Note: Of Italy's annual need for approx. 12 million tons of coal, three-quarters was shipped to Italy from Germany. It was reported that because of British interference, Italy received only half of the needed amounts of coal for domestic consumption alone—source: "Italy's Coal Dilemma" in *The Economist*. Jan 20, 1940 and the *New York Times* of January 26, 1940.

[248] *FRUS* 1940 Vol. I Welles message from Rome of March 16, 1940 (p. 98)

[249] Welles. *The Time for Decision* (p. 137)

[250] This picture is hard to find, but it does exist in the records of the French magazine *L'Illustration*. It is confirmed by a source outside of Europe in the US *Department of State Bulletin* Vol. II (p. 367) Note: Welles never mentions this incident in his memoirs *The Time for Decision*, the published version of his notes on the mission. In the original notes no mention is made either. However, the absence of the story means little, when one considers the fact that his notes indicate that he had only met with Paul Reynaud once, in his hotel during his return trip to Rome. The problem with this story is that the picture of Welles and Reynaud, and the peculiar map, was clearly *not* taken in any Hotel.

[251] Note: Roosevelt said at the Feb. 10, 1940, press conference announcing Welles' mission: "Statements made to him [Welles] by officials of governments will be kept in the strictest conficence." —source: The *Department of State Bulletin* 1940 Vol. II no. 33 (p. 155). The official British history of the Second World War demonstrates that Welles shared vital information gleaned from his meetings with Hitler and Mussolini with Chamberlain. The above-mentioned *Department of State Bulletin* reads: "Mr. Welles said that Mussolini wanted to keep out of the war, but felt that it would be difficult for him to do so; therefore he wished to end the war." Woodward's *British Foreign Policy in the Second World* War (p. 168) reads that Chamberlain was told by Welles that he believed Hitler had "a lurking want of confidence at the bottom of his mind." See also Lamb's *The Ghosts of Peace* (p. 135)

[252] Ivan Maisky's Memoirs (p.65)

[253] *Dokumente zur Deutschlandpolitik*. March 13, 1940: "Secret Prime Minister's Impressions of Mr. Welles' Visit to Europe." (p. 136)

[254] *Dokumente zur Deutschlandpolitik* No. 274 of March 13, 1940: Halifax to Lord Lothian in Washington (p. 140)

[255] *FRUS* 1940 Vol. I From Welles in Rome, March 16, 1940; the Ciano Diaries Vol. I. Entry of March 17, 1940 (p. 223); Welles, *The Time for Decision* (p.141)

[256] *Department of State Bulletin* of June 15, 1940. Vol. II no. 51, pub. 1476 (p.635)

[257] *Department of State Bulletin*. Vol. II. (p. 335) Statement of President Roosevelt, March 29, 1940

[258] The FDR Library online archive: http://www.fdrlibrary.marist.edu/psf/box6/t73aa02.html

[259] Schechter and Luchkov's *Khrushchev Remembers*. Boston, 1990 (p. 50)

[260] Note: Back on March 28, 1940, at a meeting of the Supreme Allied War Council, a "solemn agreement" was made that Britain and France would not make a separate peace or armistice. —source: *The Memoirs of General Lord Ismay*. The Viking Press: New York, 1960 (p. 102)

[261] *PREM 3*, Roll 188/2 (p. 1) Alexander Library Archives, Rutgers, the State University.

[262] *PREM 3*, Roll 188/2 (p.3)

[263] *Cadogan Diaries*: Alexander Cadogan's July 11, 1940 diary entry indicates that Halifax had such an inclination.

[264] *PRO.* Cabinet War Minutes (40) 1939, 65/13. Meeting of May 25, 26, 1940. and *PRO.* Cabinet War Minutes (40) 142nd's Conclusions: Confidential Annex.

[265] Cordell Hull Memoirs. Vol. I (p. 782)

[266] John Costello. *Ten Days to Destiny* (p. 259)

[267] British Foreign Office: USA Correspondence. F.O. 371, 1940, Vol. 24233 (p. 132) to Vol. 24234-end. Reel no. 6. Decipher no. 689—from Lothian. May 10, 1940: "Weekly Political Summary."

[268] Ibid. Reel no. 6, May 18, 1940. Doc. No, 760

[269] British Foreign Office: USA Correspondence. F.O. 371, 1940, Vol. 24233 (p. 132) to Vol. 24234-end. Reel no. 6. June 21 and 22 notes to the British Foreign Office in Lothian's "Weekly Political Summary." Note: Lothian's reference to British actions against Japan on the Burma road find corroboration in the diary of Adolf Berle. The Berle diary demonstrates just how accurate Lothian was regarding his assessment of the situation. Source: *FDRL*: Berle Diary/ Box 211. May 10, 1940 entry (p.15)

[270] *Dokumente zur Deutschlandpolitik 1939-41*. Stokes Memorandum F.O. 37/24364/c7970 (p. 178)

[271] PREM 3, Roll 188/3. Secret Cipher telegram dated June 6, 1940.

[272] *Channon Diaries*. June 14, 1940 entry.

[273] *The Goebbels Diaries 1939–41*. June 16 entry.

[274] For the contents of Churchill's cable to FDR, see W.S. Churchill's *Their Finest Hour*. Vol. III (p. 160-161); for the French government's decision to request armistice terms, see Paul Reynaud's *In the Thick of the Fight* (p. 499-500)

[275] Anthony Biddle had been the US ambassador to Poland up to the time Poland went under. This is the same individual whom the Germans claimed was the insider in FDR's attempt to stiffen Polish

resistance to negotiating a deal on the Danzig-Polish Corridor question, which precipitated the German invasion of Poland. Now he found himself in remarkably similar circumstances as a special US envoy to the French government in Bordeaux, France. Biddle's cables can be accessed at the FDR online library at: http://www.fdrlibrary.marist.edu/psf/box2/t23Lo1.html and http://www.fdrlibrary.marist.edu/psf/box2/t23no2.html

[276] *Dokumente zur Deutschlandpolitik.* Memo of W. Steed (p. 192)

[277] Note: The Churchill government called for the French to continue the fight from British or French colonial territory and proposed a "Franco-British Union," replete with immediate and unconditional joint citizenship. Source: *Documents of American Foreign Relations.* Vol. II, 1940; and the *London Times* of June 18, 1940 (p.6). As for the French request to get out of its prior obligation regarding no separate armistice or peace, and Churchill's conditional response see—*Documents on American Foreign Relations.* Vol. II, 1940 (p.434-435) or the *New York Times* of June 26, 1940 (p.6); Corroboration can also be found in Paul Badouin's *The Private Diaries of Paul Baudoin.* Trans. Charles Petrie. London, 1948 (pp. 76-100) as well as *FRUS*: "Diplomatic Papers," 1940 Vol. II (pp.455-456)

[278] *FRUS*: Vol. II. 1940, Hull memo of July 27, 1940. Corroboration of the memo is found in Hull's memoirs, (p. 796)

[279] German General Brauchitsch remarked concerning Hitler's terms: "moreover, our terms are so moderate that sheer common sense ought to make them accept." In addition, Brauchitsch continues, "after ending hostilities with England" the "French coast would be occupied only to the extent absolutely necessary." Source: Telford Taylor. *The March of Conquest* (p. 320-321)

[280] *Documents on German Foreign Policy.* Vol. 9, no. 479 (p. 608-611); Paul Schmidt. *Hitler's Interpreter.* (p. 177, 179)

[281] Walter Görlitz (ed), Trans. David Irving. *In the Service of the Reich: Originally Published as the Memoirs of Field-Marshal Keitel, Chief of the German High Command, 1938–1945.* Focal Point Publications, 2003 (p. 133)

[282] The full text, *minus Hitler's preamble*, of the Franco-German Armistice can be found in the copious Yale University online library, The Avalon Project of the Yale University Law School. Online Source: http://www.yale.edu/lawweb/avalon/wwii/frgearm.htm

[283] *Documents on American Foreign Relations* (July 1939–June 1940) Vol. II (p. 436); An online version in the original Italian can be found at: http://artsweb.bham.ac.uk/vichy/govts.htm#franco-ital

[284] *Foreign Policy Bulletin.* Foreign Policy Associations: New York. Vol. XIX no. 38 of July 12, 1940—report on Churchill's speech to the House of Commons of July 4, 1940, explaining British actions against the French fleet.

[285] Cordell Hull Memoirs (p. 799)

[286] Ibid. (p. 755)

[287] *Franklin Delano Roosevelt Library (FDRL):* "Lothian Daily Military Reports." Lothian letter to FDR of July 4, 1940.

[288] British F.O.: USA Correspondence. F.O. 371, Reel no. 6, no. 760. Lothian first recognized and reported the likelihood of such a development as early as May 18, 1940, so this development was long in the waiting for Churchill. Also *New York Times* of June 20, 1940 (p.1)

[289] British F.O.: USA Correspondence. F.O. 371, Reel no. 6, no. 1058. Cable from Lothian to the British War Cabinet of June 22, 1940.

[290] Cordell Hull Memoirs (p. 810)

[291] *Documents on German Foreign Policy.* Vol. 10 no. 114; 490/232266. Telegram of July 5, 1940: Report from Schulenberg to the German Foreign Office.

[292] *The Goebbels Diaries.* June 25, 1940 entry.

[293] *Documenti Diplomatici Italiani.* Ser. 8, V. (pp. 37 & 61), June 18, 1940.

[294] *The Last European War* (p. 97)

[295] Weizsäcker Memoirs (pp. 236-237); Walter Warlimont. *Inside Hitler's Headquarters 1939–45.* (pp113-114); *Documents on German Foreign Policy.* Vol. 10 no. 220 of July 24, 1940, (p.287)

[296] Kersten Memoirs (p. 88)

[297] Hull Memoirs (p. 806)

[298] Halder Diary: June 25, 26, 30 and July 8, 11, 13, 1940 entries.

[299] Keitel Memoirs (p. 118)

[300] David Irving. *Hitler's War* (p. 125)

[301] David Irving. *Hitler's War* (p. 128)

[302] David Irving. *Hitler's War* (p. 134)

[303] R.A. Butler's *The Art of the Possible* (pp. 190-191)

[304] David Irving. *Hitler's War* (p. 134)

[305] William L. Shirer's *The Rise and the Fall of the Third Reich.* (p.746)

[306] Liddel Hart's *World War II* (p. 83). The famous British military historian cites a letter from Blumentritt of May 17, 1940, L.H. 9/24/218 KU

[307] David Irving. *Hitler's War* (p. 134)

[308] Martienssen's *Hitler and His Admirals* (p. 658). Admiral Raeder's *My Life* also includes a number of references to Hitler's reluctance to pursue a cross-channel invasion of England.

[309] *Keitel Memoirs*. Walter Görlitz (ed) Focal Point Publications, 2003 (p. 134)

[310] *Keitel Memoirs*. Walter Görlitz (ed) Focal Point Publications, 2003 (p. 140)

[311] Casil Liddel-Hart. *The German Generals Talk* (pp. 114-115). Confirmation can be found in countless sources, including, but not limited to: Adolf Galland's *The First and the Last: The Rise and Fall of the German Fighter Forces, 1938-1945* (pp. 81-82); *Documents on German Foreign Policy* Vol. 10 (p. 494); Paul Schmidt's *Hitler's Interpreter* (p. 179);

[312] Dino Alfieri. *Dictators Face to Face*. (p. 203). Alfieri's account is backed up in Cordell Hull's *Memoirs* (p. 844) and in Willi Boelke's *The Secret Conferences of Dr. Goebbels* (July 9, 1940 entry)

[313] Channon Diary of July 18, 1940.

[314] David Dilks, "Allied Leadership in the Second World War: Churchill." *Survey*. Vol. 21 Winter-Spring, 1975, (p. 21)

[315] David Dilks, "Allied Leadership in the Second World War: Churchill." *Survey*. Vol. 21 Winter-Spring, 1975, (p. 21)

[316] David Carlton. *Churchill and the Soviet Union* (p.)

[317] *Documents on German Foreign Policy*. Vol. 10 (p.124); The German White Book, No. 6 Doc. 20, appendix A44-48 (p.1-6): "Role of AVONFORCE whilst in Norway."—A version was published and distributed in the US by the German Library of Information: New York, 1940.

[318] *Documents on German Foreign Policy* Vol. 10 Tel. no. 114, 490/232266 no. 1306. Passed on and received in Berlin on July 5, 1940.

[319] *Foreign Policy Bulletin*. Vol. XIX, no. 38, July 12, 1940.

[320] Robert O. Paxton. *Vichy France: Old Guard and New Order, 1940-1944*. Alfred A. Knopf: New York, 1972 (p. 61-63)

[321] Ibid. (p. 60-61)

[322] Robert O. Paxton. *Vichy France: Old Guard and New Order, 1940-1944* (pp. 60-72)

[323] Paul Schmidt. *Hitler's Interpreter* (p.185)

[324] Paul Schmidt. *Hitler's Interpreter* (p.184) and Galaezzo Ciano's own account in *Diplomatic Papers* (pp. 375-376)

[325] Liddel-Hart's *The German Generals Talk* (pp. 114-115); William L. Shirer's *The Rise and the Fall of the Third Reich* (p.734)—General Günther Blumentritt's recollection of Hitler's meeting with von Rundsted on May 24, 1940.

[326] Willi A. Boelki. *The Secret Conferences of Dr. Goebbels*. July 7 & 9, 1940 entries.

[327] *Documents on German Foreign Policy*. Vol. 10. Telegram from the German ambassador in Spain to Ribbentrop of July 12, 1940 (p.205)

[328] Willi A. Boelke. *The Secret Conferences of Dr. Goebbels*. July 19, 1940 entry.

[329] DeWitte Pool Special Interrogation of Goring. US *National Archives*. M-679, Roll 2, p. 5 of Göring folder. Note: After Dunkirk, Ribbentrop had offered to draft a peace plan, but Hitler replied "No, I shall do that myself."—Source: David Irving's *Hitler's War* (p.127)

[330] *Keesing's Contemporary Archives*. Weekly Diary of Important World Events. Vol. IV 1940-43. Keesing's Publishing Ltd.:London. (pp.4155-4156)

[331] DeWitte Pool Special Interrogation of Dr. Paul Schmidt. US *National Archives*. Roll 3, pp.33-34 of Schmidt Folder.

[332] Channon Diary. July 19, 1940 entry.

[333] William L. Shirer's *The Rise and Fall of the Third Reich* (p.753)

[334] Hugh Trevor-Roper's *Hitler's War Directives*. New York, 1948.

[335] *Documents on German Foreign Policy, 1940*. Vol. 10 (pp. 209-211)

[336] Halder Diary of July 13, 1940. These are not notes from the meeting itself, rather they are Halder's impressions of the meeting that he penned during the evening afterwards.

[337] Peter Donnally (ed) *Mrs. Milburn's Diaries: An Englishwoman's Day-to-Day Reflections 1939-45*. Schocken: New York, 1979 (Her Friday, July 19, 1940 entry).

[338] *Documents on German Foreign Policy*. Vol. 10, 1940. Circular of the German State Secretary directed to the German missions in Europe and the US of July 19, 1940. Response: Tel. no. 165 and no. 197 of July 20, 1940, from Madrid.

[339] Ibid. no. 201 of July 21, 1940, from the German Mission in Ireland to the German Foreign Ministry.

[340] *DGFP* Vol. 10, 1940. Telegram no. 202 of July 22, 1940.

[341] Boelke's *The Secret Conferences of Dr. Goebbels.* July 22, 1940 entry.

[342] *Dokumente zur Deutschlandpolitik* 1939–41 (p. 173)

[343] *Dokumente zur Deutschlandpolitik* 1939–41(p.173): Conclusions of the British War Cabinet on "Propaganda Future Policy." July 26, 1940.

[344] Cadogan Diary entry of July 26, 1940.

[345] Weizsäcker Memoirs (p. 237)

[346] Weizsäcker Memoirs (p. 238)

[347] Note: Much is made of the British radar installations and how they were essential to tracking German air raids. Not much is made of the fact that Germany was often announcing over the radio "Here we come!" and, "Here's where we're going!" How many German pilots died as a result of this stupidity?

[348] Boelke's *The Secret Conversations of Dr. Goebbels* (p. 69-70)

[349] Note: Hitler told General von Rundstedt on July 22, 1940, that Operation Sea Lion was principally "ein Scheinmanöver." (a.k.a.— A military bluff)—source: P. Audiat *Paris Pendant la Guerre*, cited in Lukacs' *The Last European War* (p.109)

[350] Peter Young (ed) *The Illustrated Encyclopedia of World War II.* Vol. II (p.257)

[351] Field Marshal Erich von Manstein. *Lost Victories: The War Memoirs of Hitler's Most Brilliant General.* Edited and Translated by Anthony G. Powell. Presidio Press, 1994 (p.169)

[352] Alfred Rosenberg. *Myth of the Twentieth Century.* Munich, 1934 (p. 241)

Bibliography

General Works

Selig Adler. *The Uncertain Giant, 1921–1941: American Foreign Policy Between The Wars*. New York: Collier, 1965.

D. Aigner. *Das Ringen um England*. München, 1969.

Thomas A. Bailey and Paul B. Ryan. *Hitler Vs. Roosevelt: The Undeclared Naval War*. New York: Free Press, 1979.

Hanson W. Baldwin. *The Crucial Years*. New York: Harper & Row, 1976.

E. Barker. *British Policy in South East Europe in the Second World War*. New York, 1976.

Correlli Barnett, ed. *Hitler's Generals*. New York: Grove Weidenfeld, 1989.

Ray Bearse and Anthony Read. *Conspirator: The Untold Story Of Tyler Kent*. New York: Doubleday, 1991.

Andre Beaufre. *1940: The Fall of France*. New York: Alfred A. Knopf, 1968.

P.M.H. Bell. *The Origins Of The Second World War In Europe*. New York: Longman, 1986.

Nicholas Bethell. *The War Hitler Won: The Fall of Poland, September, 1939*. New York: Holt, Rinehart and Winston,1972

Michael Burleigh. *Germany Turns Eastwards*. New York: Cambridge, 1988.

James R. Butler. *Grand Strategy*. London: HMSO, 1956–1976. [Official British War History]

R.J.C. Butow. *The John Doe Associates: Backdoor Diplomacy for Peace, 1941*. Palo Alto, CA: Stanford University Press, 1974.

Peter Calvocoressi, Guy Wint, and John Pritchard. *Total War:Causes and Courses of The Second World War*. Revised Second Edition. New York: Pantheon, 1989.

John Charmley. *Chamberlain and the Lost Peace*. London: Hodder & Stoughton, 1989.

Churchill: *The End of Glory*. New York: Harcourt Brace, 1994.

Winston Churchill. *The Gathering Storm*. Houghton-Mifflin: Boston, 1948.

John Costello. *Ten Days To Destiny: The Secret Story of the Hess Peace Initiative and British Efforts to Strike a Deal with Hitler*. New York: Morrow, 1991.

Maurice Cowling. *The Impact Of Hitler: British Politics And British Policy*. Chicago: University Press of Chicago, 1975

Robert Dallek. *Franklin D. Roosevelt And American Foreign Policy1932–1945*. New York: Oxford University Press, 1979.

Robert A. Divine. *The Reluctant Belligerent*. New York: Wiley, 1965.

Robert A. Divine. *Roosevelt & World War II*. Baltimore: Johns Hopkins, 1969.

Robert A. Divine . *Second Chance: The Triumph of Internationalism in America During World War II*. New York: Atheneum, 1967.

M.K. Dziewanowski. *War at Any Price: World War II in Europe, 1939–1945*. New York, 1991.

Ladislas Farago. *The Game Of The Foxes: The Untold Story of German Espionage in the United States and Great Britain During World War II*. New York: McKay, 1971.

Herbert Feis. *Churchill Roosevelt Stalin: The War They Waged and the Peace They Sought*. Princeton: Princeton University Press, 1957.

Joachim C. Fest. *Hitler*. New York: Harcourt Brace Jovanovich,1973.

Peter Fleming. *Operation Sea Lion*. New York: Simon and Schuster,1957.

Elanor M. Gates. *End of the Affair: The Collapse of the Anglo-French Alliance, 1939–1940*. Los Angeles: University of California Press, 1981.

K. Gemzell. *Raeder, Hitler und Skandinavien*. Lund, 1965.

Martin Gilbert. *The Second World War: A Complete History*. New York: Henry Holt, 1989.

Martin Gilbert. *Winston S. Churchill: Vol. V: The Prophet of Truth 1922–1939*. Boston: Houghton Mifflin, 1977.

Martin Gilbert. *Winston S. Churchill: Vol. VI: Finist Hour 1939–1941*. Boston: Houghton Mifflin, 1983.

Martin Gilbert and Richard Gott. *The Appeasers*. Boston: Houghton Mifflin, 1963.

Anton Gill. *An Honorable Defeat: A History of German Resistance to Hitler, 1933–1945*. New York: Henry Holt, 1994.

Bertram M. Gordon. *Collaborationism In France During The Second World War*. Ithaca: Cornell, 1980

Gabriel Gorodetsky. *Stafford Cripps' Mission to Moscow 1940–42*. Cambridge U. Press: Cambridge, 1984.

John McVickar Haight, Jr. *American Aid To France 1938–1940*. New York: Atheneum, 1970.

Michael I. Handel. *War, Strategy, and Intelligence*. London: Cass, 1989.

Lord MauriceHankey. *Diplomacy by Conference: Studies in Public Affairs, 1920–1946*. London: Ernest Benn, 1946. [Minister without Portfolio Sept 1939–May 1940, Paymaster General 1941–42].

B.H. Liddell Hart. *A History of The Second World War*. New York: G.P. Putnam's, 1971.

Waldo Heinrichs. *Threshold of War: Franklin D. Roosevelt & American Entry Into World War II*. New York: Oxford, 1988.

R. Henke. *England in Hitlers Politischen Kalkul, 1935–39*. Boppard, 1973.

Trumbull Higgins. *Soft Underbelly: The Anglo-American Controversy over the Italian Campaign 1939–1945*. New York: Macmillan, 1968.

L.E. Hill, ed. *Die Weizsacker Papiere, 1933–50*. Frankfurt-am-Main, 1974.

Andreas Hillgruber. *Deutsch Grossmacht-und-Weltpolitik im 19 und 20 Jahrhundert*. Dusseldorf, 1977.

F.H. Hinsley. *British Intelligence in the Second World War: Its Influence on Strategy and Operations*. New York: Cambridge University Press, 1979–1990. 5v.

Peter Hoffmann. *The History Of The German Resistance 1933–1945*. Cambridge, MA: MIT Press, 1977.

Heinz Hohne. *Canaris: Hitler's Master Spy*. New York: Doubleday, 1979

Alistair Horne. *To Lose A Battle: France 1940*. Boston: Little,Brown, 1969.

David Irving. *Hitler's War*. New York: Viking, 1977.

David Irving. *The War Path: Hitler's Germany 1933–1939*. New York: Viking, 1978.

David Irving. *Goring: A Biography*. New York: Morrow, 1989

Eberhard Jaeckel. *Hitler's Weltanschauung: A Blueprint for Power*. Middletown, CT, 1972.

Max Jakobsen. *The Diplomacy of the Winter War*. Harvard U. Press: Cambridge, 1961.

David Kahn. *Hitler's Spies: German Military Intelligence in World War II*. New York: Macmillan, 1978.

David Kahn. *The Codebreakers*. New York: Macmillan, 1967.

Basil Karslake. *1940: The Last Act The Story of British Forces in France after Dunkirk*. Hamden, CT: Archon, 1979.

H.R. Kedward. *Occupied France: Collaboration and Resistance 1940–1944*. London: Blackwell, 1985.

John Keegan, ed. *Churchill's Generals*. New York: Grove Weiden-feld, 1991.

Robert M. Kennedy. *The German Campaign In Poland, 1939*. Washington, DC: GPO, 1956.

Warren F. Kimball. *The Most Unsordid Act: Lend-Lease 1939–1941*. Baltimore: Johns Hopkins Press, 1969.

Warren F. Kimball . *The Juggler: Franklin Roosevelt as Wartime Statesman*. Princeton: Princeton University Press, 1991.

Christoph M. Kimmich. *The Free City: Danzig and German Foreign Policy, 1919–1934*. New Haven, CT: Yale University Press, 1968

Ivone Kirkpatrick. *Mussolini: A Study In Power*. New York: Hawthorn, 1964.

Richard Lamb. *The Ghosts of Peace*. Guilford: New York, 1987.

William L. Langer and S. Everett Gleason. *Challenge To Isolation*. New York: Harper, 1952.

William L. Langer and S. Everett Gleason. *The Undeclared War 1940–1941*. New York: Harper, 1953.

Joseph Lash. *Churchill and Roosevelt 1939–41*. W.W. Norton and Co.: New York, 1976.

Anthony Lentin. *Lloyd George and the Lost Peace: From Versailles to Hitler, 1919–1940*. Pelgrave: New York, 2001.

Wolfgang Leonhard. *Betrayal: The Hitler-Stalin Pact of 1939*. New York: St. Martin's Press, 1989.

John Lukacs. *The Last European War September 1939–December 1941*. London: Routledge and Paul, 1976.

Giles MacDonogh. *A Good German: Adam von Trott zu Solz.* Woodstock, NY: The Overlook Press, 1992.

Iain MacLeod. *Neville Chamberlain.* Atheneum: New York, 1962.

Kenneth Macksey. *Invasion: The German Invasion Of England July 1940.* New York: Macmillan, 1980.

Keith Middlemas. *The Strategy of Appeasement: The British Government and Germany 1937-1939.* Chicago: Quadrangle,1972.

R.J. Minney *The Private Papers of Hore-Belisha.* Doubleday: New York, 1961.

Wolfgang Mommsen and Lothar Kettenacker, eds. *The Fascist Challenge and the Policy of Appeasement.* Boston: Allen & Unwin, 1983.

Arnold A. Offner. *The Origins of the Second World War: American Foreign Policy and World Politics, 1917–1941.* New York: Praeger, 1975.

R.A.C. Parker. *Struggle For Survival: The History of The Second World War.* New York: Oxford, 1989.

Robert O. Paxton. *Vichy France: Old Guard and New Order 1940–1944.* New York: Columbia University Press, 1972.

Richard Petrow. *The Bitter Years: The Invasion and Occupation of Denmark and Norway April 1940–May 1945.* New York: Morrow,1974.

Gilles Perrault. *The Red Orchestra.* New York: Simon and Schuster,1967.

Alfred Rosenberg. *Der Zukunftsweg einer deutschen Aussenpolitik.* Munchen, 1927.

Norman Rich. *Hitler's War Aims. Vol. 2: The Establishment of the New Order.* New York, 1974.

Harrison E. Salisbury. *The 900 Days: The Siege of Leningrad.* New York: Harper & Row, 1969.

William L. Shirer. *The Rise and Fall of The Third Reich: A History of Nazi Germany*. New York: Simon and Schuster,1960.

A.J.P. Taylor. *The Origins of The Second World War*. New York: Atheneum, 1961.

Telford Taylor. *Munich: The Price of Peace*. New York: Doubleday, 1979.

Telford Taylor. *The March of Conquest: The German Victories In Western Europe, 1940*. New York: Simon and Schuster, 1958.

Telford Taylor. *The Breaking Wave: The Second World War in the Summer of 1940*. New York: Simon and Schuster, 1968.

Ernst Topitsch. *Stalin's War: A Radical New Theory Of The Origins Of The Second World War*. New York: St. Martin's Press, 1987.

H.R. Trevor-Roper, ed. *Blitzkrieg To Defeat: Hitler's WarDirectives 1939–1945*. New York: Holt Rinehart Winston, 1964.

Henry Ashby Turner. *German Big Business & The Rise Of Hitler*. New Oxford, 1985.

I Vizulis. *The Molotov-Ribbentrop Pact: The Baltic Case*. Westport, 1988.

Gerard L. Weinberg. *The Foreign Policy of Hitler's Germany:Diplomatic Revolution in Europe, 1933–1936*. Chicago: University of Chicago Press, 1970.

Gerhard L. Weinberg. *A World At War: A Global History of World War II*. New York: Cambridge, 1994.

John Weitz. *Hitler's Diplomat: The Life and Times of Joachim von Ribbentrop*. NewYork: Ticknor & Fields, 1992.

Frederick Winterbotham. *The Nazi Connection*. NY: Harper and Row, 1978. [head, MI6 air intelligence section]

Unpublished Documentary Materials

British Foreign Office:
USA Correspondence. From F.O. 371, Reel 6. Rutgers, the State University: Alexander Library Archives.
John L. Lewis Papers 1879–1969. M–2321, Reel 1 and 2. Rutgers, the State University: Alexander Library Archives.

PRO: British Public Records Office Documents:
PREM 3: Prime Minister's Papers. Microfilm Rolls 188/2 and 188/3.
Cabinet Papers: complete classes from the CAB & PREM series in the Public Record Office. Series one PREM 3: Papers concerning Defense and Operational Subjects, 1940–1945: Winston Churchill. Marlboro, Wiltshire, England: Adam Matthew Publications, 1998.
——. ——. War Cabinet minutes, 1939–1945. 16 reels.
——. ——. War Cabinet memoranda (WP and CP series), 1939-1945. 32 reels.
——. ——. War Cabinet memoranda [WP(G) Series], 1939–1941. 5 reels.
Microfilm— Rutgers, the State University: Alexander Library Archives.

DeWitte Pool Special Interrogations. US National Archives. Microfilm: Record Group, M–679, Rolls 1,2 and 3.

Records of the German Foreign Ministry Received by the US Department of State. National Archives. Microfilm T–120, Roll 909.

National Archives Collection of Seized Enemy Records: T–84, Rolls 194, 195. Captured Records of the Research Institute of Economic Trends, Breslau. Roll 195's "Zahlen zur Entwicklung des deutschen Aussenhandels zeit kriegsbeginn" was especially helpful in understanding the German perspective on the effectiveness of Chamberlain's Peace Front strategy.

National Archives Collection of Seized Enemy Records: T–77, Roll 438, was also useful. In particular the "Führer Directives 1939–45" related to German economic conditions in 1939 and 1940.

British Ministry of Information. *Home Intelligence: Home Intelligence reports on opinion and morale, 1940–1944.* Brighton, England: Harvester Press Microform Publications, c1979. 4 reels.

Tyler Gatewood Kent. Tyler Gatewood Kent papers, 1940–1963 (inclusive). 0.5 linear ft. (1 box). [Kent was a cipher clerk working for the US government in London. He read the cables between Roosevelt and Churchill and became convinced of a conspiracy between the two leaders to get the US into the war. He made thousands of copies of original cipher translations with the intention of exposing FDR. When it was discovered what he was doing, the US government turned him over to British authorities. He was tried and found guilty of violating British government national security laws, and was imprisoned in England for 20 years].

Published Documentary Materials

Akten zur deutschen auswartigen Politik, 1918–1945. Baden-Baden: Imprimerie Nationale, 1950.[Documents of the German Foreign Office].

British documents on foreign affairs—reports and papers from the Foreign Office confidential print. Multiple volumes covering the years 1845–1950.

British and foreign state papers [serial]. London : H.M.S.O., [18 -c1977].

Winston Churchill. *Secret Session Speeches*. London and Toronto: Cassell, 1946.

Department of State Bulletins. Vol. II, 1940.

Documents on American Foreign Relations. Vols. 1-9 (1938–1947). NY: Published for Council on Foreign Relations by Simon and Schuster, n.d.

Ernest Woodward, ed. *Documents on British Foreign Policy, 1919–1939*. London: Her Majesty's Stationery Office, 1985.

Documents on German foreign policy, 1918–1945, Series D. Various Volumes, from the archives of the German Foreign Ministry. Washington, U.S. Govt. Print. Office, 1949-[1983]

Dokumente zur Deutschlandpolitik. I. Reihe/Band I. (3 September 1939 bis 31 Dezember 1949) Alfred Metzer Verlag: Frankfurt-am-Main, nd.

Elliot Roosevelt, ed. *FDR: His Personal Letters*. Vol. II. Duell, Sloan and Pearce: New York, 1947.

Foreign Policy Bulletins. Foreign Policy Associations: New York, 1940.

FRUS: Foreign Relations of the United States. Vols. I & II. Washington, DC: US Government Printing Office, 1932– .

Anthony Martienssen, ed. *Führer Conferences on Naval Affairs, 1939.* British Admiralty: London, 1948.

Felix Gilbert,ed. *Hitler Directs His War: The Secret Records of His Daily Military Conferences.* NY: Oxford University Press, 1950.

I Documenti diplomatici italiani. Roma: Libreria dello Stato, 1953– .[Italian Diplomatic Document Documents]

International Military Tribunal. Nazi Conspiracy and Aggression, Opinion and Judgment. Office of United States Chief of Counsel for Prosecution of Axis Criminality. 1947.

International Military Tribunal. The Trial of German Major War Criminals; Proceedings of the International Military Tribunal Sitting at Nuremberg, Germany, November 20, 1945 to [October 1, 1946] Taken from the Official Transcript. 1946–1951.

Hans Adolf Jacobsen, and Arthur Lee Smith. *World War II, Policy and Strategy: Selected Documents with Commentary.* Santa Barbara: Clio, 1979.

Hansard's Parliamentary Debates, House of Commons, 1938/39–1948 volumes 341-456, 5th series.

Keesing's Contemporary Archives.
http://www.keesings.com/print_products/default.asp [Keesing's Record of World Events covers every significant event around the world and since 1931 has brought the world objectively written news reports.]

Nazi Conspiracy and Aggression. Office of the US Chief of Counsel for Prosecution of Axis Criminality. 8v., 2 supp. 1946 (Nuremberg war crimes trials)

Nazi-Soviet Relations, 1939–1941: Documents from the archives of the German Foreign Office. Ed. Raymond James Sontag and James Stuart Biddie. US Dept. of State, 1948

Peace and War: US Foreign Policy 1931–41. US Gov't Printing Office: Washington, DC, 1943.

Jane Degras, ed. *Soviet Documents on Foreign Policy*. Vol. III. Octagon Books: New York, 1978

Online Primary Documents

The Avalon Project: 20th Century Documents (Yale Law School)
URL: http://www.yale.edu/lawweb/avalon/20th.htm

EuroDocs: Primary Historical Document From Western Europe—Selected Transcriptions, Facsimiles and Translations (Brigham Young University)
URL: http://library.byu.edu/~rdh/eurodocs/

German Propaganda Archive (Calvin College)
URL: http://www.calvin.edu/academic/cas/gpa/index.htm

Wartime Official Government Publications

Ministry of Foreign Affairs. *The French Yellow Book: Diplomatic Documents (1938–1939)*. NY: By authority of the French Government, Reynal and Hitchcock, 1940.

German White Book: Documents Concerning the Last Phase of the German-Polish Crisis. 1939. [pamphlet, published by the New York German Library of Information, 1940].

The German White Book No. 5 "Allied Intrigue in the Low Countries" New York German Library of Information, 1940.

Official Documents Concerning Polish-German and Polish-Soviet Relations. The Polish White Books. London, 1940.

Periodicals

"The Origins of the Cold War: Stalin, Churchill, and the Formation of the Grand Alliance" by Gabriel Gorodetsky. *Russian Review*. Vol. 47, 1988.

"The Meaning and Significance of Fascism" by Carmen Haider. *Political Science Quarterly*. Dec., 1933.

"The Race for Northern Europe" by Martii Haikio. In Nissen, Hendrik ed. *Scandinavia During World War II*. U. of Minnesota Press: Minneapolis, 1987.

"Sir Stafford Cripps as British Ambassador to Moscow, May 1940–June 1941." By H. Hanak. The English Historical Review. Vol. XCIV, 1979.

"The Nazi-Soviet Pact: A Half-Century Later" by Gerhard L. Weinberg. *Foreign Affairs*. Fall, 1989.

"Italy's Part in the European Conflict" by R.G. Woolbert in *Foreign Policy Report*. Vol. XVI no. 4 of May 1, 1940.

Reference Works

The Oxford Companion to World War II . Ed. I.C.B. Dear. Oxford; New York: Oxford University Press, 1995

Christopher Chant. *The Encyclopedia of Codenames of World War II* . London: Routledge & Kegan Paul, 1986.

Robert Goralski. *World War II Almanac, 1931–1945: A Political and Military Record*. New York: Putnam, 1981.

Frederic M. Messick. *Primary sources in European diplomacy, 1914–1945: a bibliography of published memoirs and diaries*. New York: Greenwood Press, 1987.

Christopher Tunney. *A Biographical Dictionary of World War II*. London, Dent, 1972.

Peter Young, ed. Illustrated Encyclopedia of World War II. Vol. I. H.S. Stuttman Inc.: Westport, 1966.

Elizabeth-Anne Wheal. *The Macmillan Dictionary of the Second World War*. 2d ed. London: Macmillan, 1995.

Memoirs and Diaries

Dino Alfieri. *Dictators Face to Face*. Westport CT: Greenwood Press, 1978 repr. of 1954 ed. [Alfieri was ambassador to Germany]

P. Audiat. *Paris Pendant la Guerre*. Paris, 1946

Marshal Pietro Badoglio. *Italy in the Second World War: Memories and Documents*. London and NY: Oxford University Press, 1948. [Chief of Supreme general Staff Jun–Dec 1940, head of govt July 1943–Jun 1944].

D. Barlone. *A French Officer's Diary*. Trans. L.V. Case. Cambridge U. Press: New York, 1943.

Jozef Beck. *Final Report: Diplomatic Memoirs of Colonel Jozef Beck*. New York: Robert Speller & Sons, 1957

Nicolas von Below. *At Hitler's Side: Memoirs of Hitler's Luftwaffe Adjutant.*, 1957.

Adolf Augustus Berle. *Navigating the Rapids, 1918–1971: From the Papers of Adolf A. Berle*. NY: Harcourt Brace Jovanovich, 1973.

Anthony Biddle, Jr., Edward Wynot, ed. *Poland and the Coming of the Second World War: The Diplomatic Papers of Anthony Drexel Biddle, Jr. 1937–39*. Ohio State U. Press: Columbus, 1976.

Fedor von Bock. *General Fieldmarschall Fedor von Bock: The War Diary 1939–1945*.

Willi A. Boelke. *The Secret Conferences of Dr. Goebbels*. New York, 1970.

Georges Bonnet. Le *Quai d'Orsay sous trois républiques (1870-1961)* . Fayard, 1961 & Times Press: New York, 1965.

Georges Bonnet. *Dans la Tourmente 1938–1948*. Paris, 1970..

Karl J. Burkhardt. Meine Danziger Mission 1937–39. Munich, 1960.

Galeazzo Ciano,. ed. Hugh Gibson. *The Ciano Diaries, 1939–1943*. Garden City, NY: Doubleday, 1946. [Foreign minister 1936–43, ambassador to Vatican 1943]

Galeazzo Ciano. *Ciano Diplomatic Papers*. London, 1952.

Felix Chuev,. *Molotov Remembers: Inside Kremlin Politics — Conversations with Felix Chuev*. Chicago: Ivan Dee, 1993. [Stalin's foreign minister]

Winston Churchill. *The Second World War*. 6 Vols. Boston: Houghton Mifflin, 1948–1953.

John Rupert Colville. *The Fringes of Power: Downing Street Diaries, 1939–1955*. NY: Norton, 1985. [Churchill's private secretary]

Birgher Dahlerus. *The Last Attempt*. London, 1947.

David Dilks, ed. *The Diaries of Sir Alexander Cadogan 1938–45*. New York, 1972.

P. Donnelly, ed. *Mrs. Milburn's Diaries: An Englishwoman's Day-to-Day Reflections 1939-45*. New York, 1979.

Anthony Eden. *The Eden Memoirs* (3 Vols): Facing the Dictators, The Reckoning and Full Circle. various publishers. [Secretary of State for War May–Dec 1940, Foreign Secretary 1935–38, 1940–45]

André Francois-Poncet. *The Fateful Years: Memoirs of a French Ambassador in Berlin, 1931–1938*. NY: H. Fertig, 1972.

Adolf Galland. *The First And The Last*. New York: Bantam, 1954.

Gustav-Maurice Gamelin. *Servir*. Paris, 1946–47.

Walter Gorlitz, ed.Trans. David Irving. *The Memoirs of Field-Marshal Wilhelm Keitel*. NY: Stein and Day, 2001.[Armed Forces Chief of Staff]

Heinz Guderian. *Panzer Leader*. New York: Dutton, 1951.

Georg Achates Gripenberg. *Finland and the Great Powers: Memoirs of a Diplomat*.

Georg Achates Gripenberg. *Memoirs of the Finnish Ambassador*.

Franz Halder. *The Halder Diaries: The Private War Journals of Colonel-*

General Franz Halder. 2 Volumes. Boulder, CO: Westview, 1976. [Chief of army general staff 1938–42]

Oliver Harvey. *The Diplomatic Diaries of Oliver Harvey.* London, 1970.

Ulrich von Hassell. *The Von Hassell Diaries, 1938–1944: The Story of the Forces Against Hitler Inside Germany.* London: Hamilton, 1948. [prewar ambassador to Italy, a resistance leader].

Adolf Hitler. *Mein Kampf.* Trans. Ralph Manheim. Houghton-Mifflin: Boston, 1971.

Cordell Hull. *Memoirs.* Vol. I, MacMillan: New York, 1948.

Harold L. Ickes. *The Secret Diary of Harold L. Ickes.* 3 Vols. NY: Simon and Schuster, 1953–54. [covers 1933–1941].

Robert Rhodes James, ed. *CHIPS: The Diaries of Sir Henry Channon.* Weidenfeld and Nicholson: London, 1967.

Albrecht Kesselring. *The Memoirs of Field-Marshal Kesselring.*

Erich Kordt. Wahn und Wirklichkeit. Stuttgart, 1947.

Edmund Ironside. *Time Unguarded: The Ironside Diaries, 1937–1940.* Westport CT: Greenwood Press, 1974. [Chief of the Imperial General Staff Sept 1939–May 1940].

R. Macleod and D. Kelly, eds. *Ironsides Diaries, 1937–40.* London, 1963.

Joseph Goebbels, F. Taylor, ed. *The Goebbels Diaries, 1939–1941.* 1983.

Pierre Laval. *The Diary of Pierre Laval.* New York: Scribner's and Sons, 1948.

B.H. Liddell-Hart, ed. *The Rommel Papers.* New York: Harcourt, Brace and Company, 1953.

Jozef Lipski. *Diplomat in Berlin, 1933–1939: Papers and Memoirs of Jozef Lipski, Ambassador of Poland.* NY: Columbia University Press, 1968.

Juliusz Lukasiewicz. *Diplomat in Paris, 1936-1939: Papers and Memoirs of Juliusz Lukasiewicz, Ambassador of Poland.* NY: Columbia University Press, 1970.

Sir Harold Macmillan. *The Blast of War, 1939–1945.* NY: Harper and Row, 1968.

I.M. Maisky. *Memoirs of a Soviet Ambassador: The War, 1939–1943.* NY: Scribner, 1968. [Ambassador to Britain 1932–43]

Carl Gustav Emil Mannerheim. *Memoirs.* London: Cassell, 1953. [Finnish army chief 1939–44, President f.1944].

Erich von Manstein. *Lost Victories.* Novato, CA: Presidio, 1982. [chief of staff in Poland 1939, shaped 1940 attack plan, senior general in Russia 1941–44]

H.G. Nicholas. *Despatches from Washington, 1941–1946: Weekly Political Reports from the British Embassy.* Chicago: University of Chicago Press, 1981.

Sir Harold Nicolson. *Diaries and Letters.* 3 vols. NY: Atheneum, 1966–68. [vol.II deals with World War II). [MP and Parliamentary Secretary to Min. of Information 1940–41].

Franz von Papen, *Memoirs.* NY: Dutton, 1953. [Ambassador to Austria 1934–38, to Turkey 1939–44]

Erich Raeder. *My Life.* Trans. Henry W. Drexel. Banta Books: Annapolis, 1960. [Navy C-in-C 1928–43, Navy Inspector-General f.1943]

Paul Reynaud. In the Thick of the Fight. New York, 1965. [Head of French Ministry of Economics and French Premier after Daladier's dismissal].

Joachim von Ribbentrop. *The Ribbentrop Memoirs*, translated by Alan Bullock. London: Weidenfeld and Nicolson, 1954.

Friedrich Ruge. *The German Navy's Story: 1939–45.* Trans. Commander M.G. Sounders. US Naval Institute: Annapolis, 1963. [Vice admiral of the German navy]

Dr. Paul Schmidt. Hitler's Interpreter. Ed. RHC Steed. MacMillan: New York, 1951.

Sir Edward Spears. *Assignment to Catastrophe*. 2 Vols. NY: A.A. Wyn, 1954–55. [Churchill's personal representative to French PM Reynaud 1940; vols. deal with France 1939–June 1940]

Albert Speer. *Inside The Third Reich*. New York: Macmillan, 1970.

Albert Speer. *Spandau: The Secret Diaries*. New York: Macmillan, 1976

Henry Ashby Turner., ed. *Hitler: Memoirs of a Confidant*. New Haven: Yale University Press, 1985.

Walter Schellenberg. *Hitler's Secret Service*. New York: Pyramid, 1956.

J.L. Schecter and V.V. Luchkov. *Khrushchev Remembers*. Boston, 1990.

Alexander Stahlberg. *Bounded Duty; The Memoirs of a German Officer 1932–45*. New York: Brassey's, 1990.

Henry Louis Stimson.. *On Active Service in Peace and War*. NY: Harper, 1948. [Secretary of War 1940–1945 under FDR and Truman]

Paval Sudoplatov and Anatoli Sudoplatov. *Special Tasks: The Memoirs Of An Unwanted Witness—A Soviet Spymaster*. Boston: Little, Brown, 1994.

Raoul Wallenberg. *Letters and Dispatches, 1924–1944*. Tr. Kjersti Board. Arcade Publishing, 1995.

Walther Warlimont. *Inside Hitler's Headquarters 1939–45*. New York: Praeger, 1964 [Planning Chief of the Wehrmacht General Staff]

Ernst von Weizsäcker. *Memoirs*. Trans. John Andrews. Henry Regnery: New York, 1951.

Sumner Welles. *The Time for Decision*. Harper and Brothers: New York, 1944.

G.V. Zhukov. *The Memoirs of Marshal Zhukov*. Delacorte: New York

Printed in the United States
38992LVS00005B/346-360

9 781413 748291